Super Easy Ninja Dual Zone

Air Fryer

Cookbook 2023

1800+ Days Delicious, Energy-saving & Crispy Recipes Book for Beginners with Tips & Tricks - UK Measurements & Ingredients

Annabel Komine

Table of Contents

Chapter 4 Poultry   25

Chapter 5 Fish and Seafood   33

Chapter 6 Snacks and Appetizers   40

Chapter 7 Vegetables and Sides 47

Chapter 8 Vegetarian Mains 54

Chapter 9 Family Favorites 58

Chapter 10 Fast and Easy Everyday Favourites 62

INTRODUCTION

Air frying has taken the culinary world by storm, revolutionizing the way we cook and enjoy our favorite foods. Imagine indulging in crispy, golden fries or perfectly cooked chicken wings without the guilt of excessive oil. With the Ninja Dual Zone Air Fryer, this dream becomes a delicious reality.

Welcome to the Ninja Dual Zone Air Fryer Cookbook, where we embark on a culinary adventure together, exploring the art of air frying and harnessing the power of this incredible kitchen appliance. This cookbook is designed to be your comprehensive guide, providing you with expert techniques, mouthwatering recipes, and invaluable tips to create exceptional meals with your Ninja Dual Zone Air Fryer.

Air frying has gained immense popularity in recent years, and for good reason. Not only does it offer a healthier alternative to traditional frying methods, but it also delivers outstanding results. Air frying requires little to no oil, significantly reducing the fat content of your dishes, while still achieving that desired crispy texture. It's a game-changer for those who crave delicious fried foods without compromising on their well-being. Plus, the convenience and versatility of air frying make it a go-to cooking method for busy individuals and families alike.

At the heart of this cookbook lies the Ninja Dual Zone Air Fryer—a cutting-edge appliance that takes air frying to a whole new level. Its dual independent cooking zones provide you with unprecedented flexibility and efficiency in the kitchen. No longer do you have to wait for one dish to finish cooking before starting another. With the dual zones, you can simultaneously cook two different dishes without any flavor transfer. It's like having two air fryers in one, allowing you to prepare complete meals with ease.

The Ninja Dual Zone Air Fryer Cookbook is your ultimate resource for maximizing the potential of this remarkable appliance. From appetizers and snacks to main courses and desserts, we will explore a wide range of recipes that showcase the versatility and capabilities of your air fryer. But this cookbook is more than just recipes; it's a comprehensive guide that will empower you with the knowledge and skills to become an air frying master.

Throughout the following chapters, we will delve into the essential techniques and tips to achieve air frying success. We'll uncover the optimal cooking temperatures for different types of food, guide you on arranging your ingredients within the cooking zones for even cooking, and show you how to enhance flavors using marinades, spices, and coatings. You'll also learn how to properly care for and maintain your Ninja Dual Zone Air Fryer to ensure its longevity and peak performance.

So, get ready to embark on a culinary adventure like no other. Let the Ninja Dual Zone Air Fryer Cookbook be your guide as we unlock the full potential of your air fryer and create tantalizing dishes that will impress your family and friends. The world of air frying awaits, and together, we'll master the art of crispy, delicious meals with ease.

The Rise of Air Frying

Air frying is not just a passing trend; it has solid roots in the culinary world. The concept of air frying originated in the 1970s when a German company introduced the first air fryer for commercial use. However, it wasn't until recent years that air frying truly gained widespread recognition and popularity. As people became more health-conscious and sought ways to enjoy their favorite fried foods with fewer calories and less fat, air frying emerged as the perfect solution. Today, air frying has become a kitchen staple for health-conscious individuals and food enthusiasts alike.

Air frying offers a multitude of benefits that have contributed to its surge in popularity. One of the main advantages is the healthier approach to cooking. By using hot air circulation and minimal or no oil, air frying reduces the amount of unhealthy fats and calories in your favorite fried dishes. It allows you to enjoy the satisfying crunch and texture of fried foods without sacrificing your health.

Moreover, air frying delivers consistently crispy and evenly cooked results. The hot air circulates around the food, creating a golden-brown exterior while maintaining moisture inside. Whether you're cooking French fries, chicken wings, or even doughnuts, air frying ensures a delightful crunch without the greasy residue.

The convenience of air frying is another factor that has propelled its rise. Unlike traditional frying methods that involve messy oil splatters and monitoring precise temperatures, air frying simplifies the process. With pre-set cooking times and temperatures, you can achieve excellent results with just a few button presses. Plus, the quick cooking times of air frying mean you can enjoy your favorite dishes in a fraction of the time it would take using other cooking methods.

Air frying is not limited to specific types of food—it is remarkably versatile. You can air fry a wide array of dishes, from appetizers and snacks to main courses and even desserts. Crispy chicken tenders, roasted vegetables, homemade potato chips, and even chocolate chip cookies can all be prepared using the air fryer. This versatility opens up endless possibilities in the kitchen, allowing you to experiment with different flavors, textures, and culinary creations.

The rise of air frying can be attributed to its appeal as a healthier cooking method, the ability to achieve crispy results without excess oil, and the convenience and versatility it offers in the kitchen. As we delve further into this cookbook, you'll discover the incredible potential of the Ninja Dual Zone Air Fryer and how it harnesses the power of air frying to create delicious, guilt-free meals. So, let's continue our journey and uncover the secrets to mastering the art of air frying with your Ninja Dual Zone Air Fryer.

Get Ready to Cook

Before diving into the recipes and techniques, it's essential to familiarize yourself with the Ninja Dual Zone Air Fryer. Take a moment to explore its features, controls, and settings. Get to know the layout of the dual independent cooking zones, the temperature and time controls, as well as any additional functions or accessories that come with your air fryer. Understanding the equipment you'll be working with is crucial for successful and enjoyable cooking experiences.

Creating a well-prepared cooking space will make your air frying experience smoother and more efficient. Clear your countertop of any unnecessary clutter and ensure you have enough space for the air fryer to sit securely. Make sure there's a nearby power outlet for easy access. Gather your cooking utensils, measuring cups, and any other tools you may need. Having everything within reach will streamline your cooking process and prevent unnecessary interruptions.

Browse through the recipes included in this cookbook and select the dishes you'd like to prepare. Take note of the ingredients required for each recipe and make a comprehensive shopping list. Ensure you have all the necessary ingredients on hand before you begin cooking. Organize your ingredients in a tidy and accessible manner, grouping them according to their use in different recipes. This way, you'll have everything readily available when it's time to start cooking.

Safety should always be a priority in the kitchen. Familiarize yourself with the safety guidelines provided by the manufacturer for your Ninja Dual Zone Air Fryer. Pay attention to recommended cooking temperatures, handling hot surfaces, and proper use of the cooking baskets and accessories. Make sure your air fryer is placed on a stable surface, away from any flammable materials. Additionally, keep children and pets away from the cooking area to prevent accidents. By adhering to safety guidelines, you can enjoy cooking with peace of mind.

Now that you've familiarized yourself with the Ninja Dual Zone Air Fryer, prepared your cooking space, gathered your ingredients, and reviewed the safety guidelines, you're ready to embark on an exciting cooking journey. The recipes and techniques in this cookbook will help you unlock the full potential of your air fryer and create mouthwatering meals that will delight your taste buds. Get ready to explore a world of flavors, experiment with different ingredients, and elevate your culinary skills with the Ninja Dual Zone Air Fryer.

As you prepare to cook, remember to approach each recipe with enthusiasm and an open mind. Don't be afraid to make modifications or add your personal touch to the dishes. The joy of cooking lies in the creativity and enjoyment it brings. So, get ready to embark on a culinary adventure, armed with your Ninja Dual Zone Air Fryer and the invaluable knowledge and recipes provided in this cookbook. It's time to unleash your inner chef and create culinary masterpieces that will impress both yourself and those fortunate enough to taste your creations. Happy cooking!

Chapter 1 Breakfasts

Chapter 1 Breakfasts

Smoky Sausage Patties

Prep time: 30 minutes | Cook time: 9 minutes | Serves 8

450 g pork mince	½ teaspoon fennel seeds
1 tablespoon soy sauce or tamari	½ teaspoon dried thyme
1 teaspoon smoked paprika	½ teaspoon freshly ground black pepper
1 teaspoon dried sage	¼ teaspoon cayenne pepper
1 teaspoon sea salt	

1. In a large bowl, combine the pork, soy sauce, smoked paprika, sage, salt, fennel seeds, thyme, black pepper, and cayenne pepper. Work the meat with your hands until the seasonings are fully incorporated. 2. Shape the mixture into 8 equal-size patties. Using your thumb, make a dent in the center of each patty. Place the patties on a plate and cover with plastic wrap. Refrigerate the patties for at least 30 minutes. 3. Working in batches if necessary, place the patties in a single layer half in zone 1, the remaining in zone 2. Being careful not to overcrowd them. 4. Set the air fryer to 200°C and air fry for 5 minutes. Flip and cook for about 4 minutes more.

Classic British Breakfast & Breakfast Sausage and Cauliflower

Prep time: 10 minutes | Cook time: 45 minutes

Classic British Breakfast	Serves 2:	450 g sausage meat, cooked and crumbled
235 g potatoes, sliced and diced	475 ml double/whipping cream
475 g baked beans	1 head cauliflower, chopped
2 eggs	235 g grated Cheddar cheese, plus more for topping
1 tablespoon rapeseed oil	
1 sausage	8 eggs, beaten
Salt, to taste	Salt and ground black pepper, to taste
Breakfast Sausage and Cauliflower	Serves 4:	

Prepare for Classic British Breakfast:
1. Preheat the air fryer to 200°C and allow to warm.
2. Break the eggs onto a baking dish and sprinkle with salt.
3. Lay the beans on the dish, next to the eggs.
4. In a bowl, coat the potatoes with the rapeseed oil. Sprinkle with salt.
5. Transfer the bowl of potato slices to zone 1.
Prepare for Breakfast Sausage and Cauliflower:
1. Preheat zone 2 to 180°C.
2. In a large bowl, mix the sausage, cream, chopped cauliflower, cheese and eggs. Sprinkle with salt and ground black pepper.
3. Pour the mixture into a greased casserole dish in zone 2.
Cook:
1. In zone 1, adjust the air fryer temperature to 200°C and air fry for 10 minutes.
2. In zone 2, adjust the air fryer temperature to 180°C and air fry for 45 minutes.
3. Press SYNC, then press Start.
4. For zone 1, swap out the bowl of potatoes for the dish containing the eggs and beans. Bake for another 10 minutes. Cover the potatoes with parchment paper. Slice up the sausage and throw the slices on top of the beans and eggs. Bake for another 5 minutes. Serve with the potatoes.
5. For zone 2, top with more Cheddar cheese and serve.

Cajun Breakfast Sausage

Prep time: 10 minutes | Cook time: 15 to 20 minutes | Serves 8

680 g 85% lean turkey mince	1 teaspoon Cajun seasoning
3 cloves garlic, finely chopped	1 teaspoon dried thyme
¼ onion, grated	½ teaspoon paprika
1 teaspoon Tabasco sauce	½ teaspoon cayenne

1. Preheat the air fryer to 190°C. 2. In a large bowl, combine the turkey, garlic, onion, Tabasco, Cajun seasoning, thyme, paprika, and cayenne. Mix with clean hands until thoroughly combined. Shape into 16 patties, about ½ inch thick. (Wet your hands slightly if you find the sausage too sticky to handle.) 3. Working in batches if necessary, arrange the patties in a single layer half in zone 1, the remaining in zone 2. Pausing halfway through the cooking time to flip the patties, air fry for 15 to 20 minutes until a thermometer inserted into the thickest portion registers 74°C.

Spinach and Mushroom Mini Quiche

Prep time: 10 minutes | Cook time: 15 minutes | Serves 4

1 teaspoon rapeseed oil, plus more for spraying	4 eggs, beaten
235 g roughly chopped mushrooms	120 g grated Cheddar cheese
235 g fresh baby spinach, grated	120 g grated Cheddar cheese
	¼ teaspoon salt
	¼ teaspoon black pepper

1. Spray 4 silicone baking cups with rapeseed oil and set aside. 2. In a medium sauté pan over medium heat, warm 1 teaspoon of rapeseed oil. Add the mushrooms and sauté until soft, 3 to 4 minutes. 3. Add the spinach and cook until wilted, 1 to 2 minutes. Set aside. 4. In a medium bowl, whisk together the eggs, Cheddar cheese, Cheddar cheese, salt, and pepper. 5. Gently fold the mushrooms and spinach into the egg mixture. 6. Pour ¼ of the mixture into each silicone baking cup. 7. Place the baking cups into one of the air fryer baskets and air fry at 180ºC for 5 minutes. Stir the mixture in each ramekin slightly and air fry until the egg has set, an additional 3 to 5 minutes.

Hearty Cheddar Biscuits

Prep time: 10 minutes | Cook time: 22 minutes | Makes 8 biscuits

250 g self-raising flour	plus more to melt on top
2 tablespoons sugar	315 ml buttermilk
120 g butter, frozen for 15 minutes	235 g plain flour, for shaping
120 g grated Cheddar cheese,	1 tablespoon butter, melted

1. Line a buttered 7-inch metal cake pan with parchment paper or a silicone liner. 2. Combine the flour and sugar in a large mixing bowl. Grate the butter into the flour. Add the grated cheese and stir to coat the cheese and butter with flour. Then add the buttermilk and stir just until you can no longer see streaks of flour. The dough should be quite wet. 3. Spread the plain (not self-raising) flour out on a small cookie sheet. With a spoon, scoop 8 evenly sized balls of dough into the flour, making sure they don't touch each other. With floured hands, coat each dough ball with flour and toss them gently from hand to hand to shake off any excess flour. Put each floured dough ball into the prepared pan, right up next to the other. This will help the biscuits rise, rather than spreading out. 4. Preheat the air fryer to 190ºC. 5. Transfer the cake pan to the basket of the air fryer. Let the ends of the aluminum foil sling hang across the cake pan before returning the basket to the air fryer. 6. Air fry for 20 minutes. Check the biscuits twice to make sure they are not getting too brown on top. If they are, re-arrange the aluminum foil strips to cover any brown parts. After 20 minutes, check the biscuits by inserting a toothpick into the center of the biscuits. It should come out clean. If it needs a little more time, continue to air fry for two extra minutes. Brush the tops of the biscuits with some melted butter and sprinkle a little more grated cheese on top if desired. Pop the basket back into the air fryer for another 2 minutes. 7. Remove the cake pan from the air fryer. Let the biscuits cool for just a minute or two and then turn them out onto a plate and pull apart. Serve immediately.

Pancake Cake & Jalapeño and Bacon Breakfast Pizza

Prep time: 15 minutes | Cook time: 10 minutes

Pancake Cake	Serves 4:	½ teaspoon ground cinnamon
60 g blanched finely ground almond flour	Jalapeño and Bacon Breakfast Pizza	Serves 2:
30 g powdered erythritol	235 ml grated Cheddar cheese
½ teaspoon baking powder	30 g soft cheese, broken into small pieces
2 tablespoons unsalted butter, softened	4 slices cooked bacon, chopped
1 large egg	60 g chopped pickled jalapeños
½ teaspoon unflavoured gelatin	1 large egg, whisked
½ teaspoon vanilla extract	¼ teaspoon salt

Prepare for Pancake Cake:
1. In a large bowl, mix almond flour, erythritol, and baking powder. Add butter, egg, gelatin, vanilla, and cinnamon. Pour into a round baking pan.
2. Place pan into zone 1.
Prepare for Jalapeño and Bacon Breakfast Pizza:
1. Place Mozzarella in a single layer on the bottom of an ungreased round nonstick baking dish. Scatter soft cheese pieces, bacon, and jalapeños over Mozzarella, then pour egg evenly around baking dish.
2. Sprinkle with salt and place into zone 2.
Cook:
1. In zone 1, adjust the air fryer temperature to 150ºC and air fry for 7 minutes.
2. In zone 2, adjust the air fryer temperature to 170ºC and air fry for 10 minutes.
3. Press SYNC, then press Start.
4. For zone 1, when the cake is completely cooked, a toothpick will come out clean. Cut cake into four and serve.
5. For zone 2,when cheese is brown and egg is set, pizza will be done. Let cool on a large plate 5 minutes before serving.

Spinach and Swiss Frittata with Mushrooms

Prep time: 10 minutes | Cook time: 20 minutes |
Serves 4

rapeseed oil cooking spray	110 g baby mushrooms, sliced
8 large eggs	1 shallot, diced
½ teaspoon salt	120 g grated Swiss cheese,
½ teaspoon black pepper	divided
1 garlic clove, minced	Hot sauce, for serving (optional)
475 g fresh baby spinach	

1. Preheat the air fryer to 180ºC. Lightly coat the inside of a 6-inch round cake pan with rapeseed oil cooking spray. 2. In a large bowl, beat the eggs, salt, pepper, and garlic for 1 to 2 minutes, or until well combined. 3. Fold in the spinach, mushrooms, shallot, and 60 ml the Swiss cheese. 4. Pour the egg mixture into the prepared cake pan, and sprinkle the remaining 60 ml Swiss over the top. 5. Place into the air fryer and bake for 18 to 20 minutes, or until the eggs are set in the center. 6. Remove from the air fryer and allow to cool for 5 minutes. Drizzle with hot sauce (if using) before serving.

Easy Sausage Pizza & Bourbon Vanilla French Toast

Prep time: 25 minutes | Cook time: 6 minutes

Easy Sausage Pizza	Serves 4:	2 tablespoons water
2 tablespoons ketchup	160 ml whole or semi-skimmed
1 pitta bread	milk
80 g sausage meat	1 tablespoon butter, melted
230 g Cheddar cheese	2 tablespoons bourbon
1 teaspoon garlic powder	1 teaspoon vanilla extract
1 tablespoon rapeseed oil	8 (1-inch-thick) French bread
Bourbon Vanilla French Toast		slices
Serves 4:	Cooking spray
2 large eggs	

Prepare for Easy Sausage Pizza:
1. Preheat the air fryer to 170ºC.
2. Spread the ketchup over the pitta bread.
3. Top with the sausage meat and cheese. Sprinkle with the garlic powder and rapeseed oil.
4. Put the pizza in zone 1.
Prepare for Bourbon Vanilla French Toast:
1. Preheat the air fryer to 160ºC. Line zone 2 with parchment paper and spray it with cooking spray.
2. Beat the eggs with the water in a shallow bowl until combined. Add the milk, melted butter, bourbon, and vanilla and stir to mix well.

3. Dredge 4 slices of bread in the batter, turning to coat both sides evenly. Transfer the bread slices onto the parchment paper.
Cook:
1. In zone 1, adjust the air fryer temperature to 170ºC and air fry for 6 minutes.
2. In zone 2, adjust the air fryer temperature to 160ºC and air fry for 6minutes.
3. Press SYNC, then press Start.
4. For zone 2, flip the slices halfway through the cooking time. Remove from the basket to a plate and repeat with the remaining 4 slices of bread. Serve warm.

Sausage and Cheese Balls

Prep time: 10 minutes | Cook time: 12 minutes |
Makes 16 balls

450 g pork sausage meat,	30 g full-fat soft cheese,
removed from casings	softened
120 g grated Cheddar cheese	1 large egg

1. Mix all ingredients in a large bowl. Form into sixteen (1-inch) balls. Place the balls into one of the air fryer baskets. 2. Adjust the temperature to 200ºC and air fry for 12 minutes. 3. Shake the basket two or three times during cooking. Sausage balls will be browned on the outside and have an internal temperature of at least 64ºC when completely cooked. 4. Serve warm.

Lemon-Blueberry Muffins

Prep time: 5 minutes | Cook time: 20 to 25 minutes |
Makes 6

muffins	2 large eggs
150 g almond flour	3 tablespoons melted butter
3 tablespoons granulated	1 tablespoon almond milk
sweetener	1 tablespoon fresh lemon juice
1 teaspoon baking powder	120 g fresh blueberries

1. Preheat the air fryer to 180ºC. Lightly coat 6 silicone muffin cups with vegetable oil. Set aside. 2. In a large mixing bowl, combine the almond flour, sweetener, and baking soda. Set aside. 3. In a separate small bowl, whisk together the eggs, butter, milk, and lemon juice. Add the egg mixture to the flour mixture and stir until just combined. Fold in the blueberries and let the batter sit for 5 minutes. 4. Spoon the muffin batter into the muffin cups, about two-thirds full. Air fry for 20 to 25 minutes, or until a toothpick inserted into the center of a muffin comes out clean. 5. Remove the basket from the air fryer and let the muffins cool for about 5 minutes before transferring them to a wire rack to cool completely.

Bacon-and-Eggs Avocado

Prep time: 5 minutes | Cook time: 17 minutes | Serves 1

1 large egg
1 avocado, halved, peeled, and pitted
2 slices bacon
Fresh parsley, for serving (optional)
Sea salt flakes, for garnish (optional)

1. Spray one of the air fryer baskets with avocado oil. Preheat the air fryer to 160°C. Fill a small bowl with cool water. 2. Soft-boil the egg: Place the egg in one of the air fryer baskets. Air fry for 6 minutes for a soft yolk or 7 minutes for a cooked yolk. Transfer the egg to the bowl of cool water and let sit for 2 minutes. Peel and set aside. 3. Use a spoon to carve out extra space in the center of the avocado halves until the cavities are big enough to fit the soft-boiled egg. Place the soft-boiled egg in the center of one half of the avocado and replace the other half of the avocado on top, so the avocado appears whole on the outside. 4. Starting at one end of the avocado, wrap the bacon around the avocado to completely cover it. Use cocktail sticks to hold the bacon in place. 5. Place the bacon-wrapped avocado in the air fryer basket and air fry for 5 minutes. Flip the avocado over and air fry for another 5 minutes, or until the bacon is cooked to your liking. Serve on a bed of fresh parsley, if desired, and sprinkle with salt flakes, if desired. 6. Best served fresh. Store extras in an airtight container in the fridge for up to 4 days. Reheat in a preheated 160°C air fryer for 4 minutes, or until heated through.

Red Pepper and Feta Frittata

Prep time: 10 minutes | Cook time: 20 minutes | Serves 4

rapeseed oil cooking spray
8 large eggs
1 medium red pepper, diced
½ teaspoon salt
½ teaspoon black pepper
1 garlic clove, minced
120 g feta, divided

1. Preheat the air fryer to 180°C. Lightly coat the inside of a 6-inch round cake pan with rapeseed oil cooking spray. 2. In a large bowl, beat the eggs for 1 to 2 minutes, or until well combined. 3. Add the red pepper, salt, black pepper, and garlic to the eggs, and mix together until the red pepper is distributed throughout. 4. Fold in 60 ml the feta cheese. 5. Pour the egg mixture into the prepared cake pan, and sprinkle the remaining 60 ml feta over the top. 6. Place into the air fryer and bake for 18 to 20 minutes, or until the eggs are set in the center. 7. Remove from the air fryer and allow to cool for 5 minutes before serving.

Portobello Eggs Benedict

Prep time: 10 minutes | Cook time: 10 to 14 minutes | Serves 2

1 tablespoon rapeseed oil
2 cloves garlic, minced
¼ teaspoon dried thyme
2 portobello mushrooms, stems removed and gills scraped out
2 vine tomatoes, halved lengthwise
Salt and freshly ground black
pepper, to taste
2 large eggs
2 tablespoons grated Pecorino Romano cheese
1 tablespoon chopped fresh parsley, for garnish
1 teaspoon truffle oil (optional)

1. Preheat the air fryer to 200°C. 2. In a small bowl, combine the rapeseed oil, garlic, and thyme. Brush the mixture over the mushrooms and tomatoes until thoroughly coated. Season to taste with salt and freshly ground black pepper. 3. Arrange the vegetables, cut side up, in one of the air fryer baskets. Crack an egg into the center of each mushroom and sprinkle with cheese. Air fry for 10 to 14 minutes until the vegetables are tender and the whites are firm. When cool enough to handle, coarsely chop the tomatoes and place on top of the eggs. Scatter parsley on top and drizzle with truffle oil, if desired, just before serving.

Mississippi Spice Muffins

Prep time: 15 minutes | Cook time: 13 minutes | Makes 12 muffins

1 kg plain
1 tablespoon ground cinnamon
2 teaspoons baking soda
2 teaspoons allspice
1 teaspoon ground cloves
1 teaspoon salt
235 g (2 sticks) butter, room
temperature
350 g sugar
2 large eggs, lightly beaten
475 ml unsweetened applesauce
60 g chopped pecans
1 to 2 tablespoons oil

1. In a large bowl, whisk the flour, cinnamon, baking soda, allspice, cloves, and salt until blended. 2. In another large bowl, combine the butter and sugar. Using an electric mixer, beat the mixture for 2 to 3 minutes until light and fluffy. Add the beaten eggs and stir until blended. 3. Add the flour mixture and applesauce, alternating between the two and blending after each addition. Stir in the pecans. 4. Preheat the air fryer to 160°C. Spritz 12 silicone muffin cups with oil. 5. Pour the batter into the prepared muffin cups, filling each halfway. Place the muffins in one of the air fryer baskets. 6. Air fry for 6 minutes. Shake the basket and air fry for 7 minutes more. The muffins are done when a toothpick inserted into the middle comes out clean.

Cinnamon Rolls

600 g grated Cheddar cheese	½ teaspoon vanilla extract
60 g soft cheese, softened	96 ml icing sugar-style
120 g blanched finely ground	sweetener
almond flour	1 tablespoon ground cinnamon

1. In a large microwave-safe bowl, combine Cheddar cheese, soft cheese, and flour. Microwave the mixture on high 90 seconds until cheese is melted. 2. Add vanilla extract and sweetener, and mix 2 minutes until a dough forms. 3. Once the dough is cool enough to work with your hands, about 2 minutes, spread it out into a 12 × 4-inch rectangle on ungreased parchment paper. Evenly sprinkle dough with cinnamon. 4. Starting at the long side of the dough, roll lengthwise to form a log. Slice the log into twelve even pieces. 5. Divide rolls between two ungreased round nonstick baking dishes. Place one dish into air fryer basket. Adjust the temperature to 190ºC and bake for 10 minutes. 6. Cinnamon rolls will be done when golden around the edges and mostly firm. Repeat with second dish. Allow rolls to cool in dishes 10 minutes before serving.

Turkey Sausage Breakfast Pizza

4 large eggs, divided	120 g grated low-moisture
1 tablespoon water	Mozzarella or other melting
½ teaspoon garlic powder	cheese
½ teaspoon onion granules	1 link cooked turkey sausage,
½ teaspoon dried oregano	chopped (about 60 g)
2 tablespoons coconut flour	2 sun-dried tomatoes, finely
3 tablespoons grated Parmesan	chopped
cheese	2 sping onions, thinly sliced

1. Preheat the air fryer to 200ºC. Line a cake pan with parchment paper and lightly coat the paper with rapeseed oil. 2. In a large bowl, whisk 2 of the eggs with the water, garlic powder, onion granules, and dried oregano. Add the coconut flour, breaking up any lumps with your hands as you add it to the bowl. Stir the coconut flour into the egg mixture, mixing until smooth. Stir in the Parmesan cheese. Allow the mixture to rest for a few minutes until thick and dough-like. 3. Transfer the mixture to the prepared pan. Use a spatula to spread it evenly and slightly up the sides of the pan. Air fry until the crust is set but still light in color, about 10 minutes. Top with the cheeses, sausage, and sun-dried tomatoes. 4. Break the remaining 2 eggs into a small bowl, then slide them onto the pizza. Return the pizza to the air fryer. Air fry 10 to 14 minutes until the egg whites are set and the yolks are the desired doneness. Top with the scallions and allow to rest for 5 minutes before serving.

Blueberry Cobbler

40 g wholemeal pastry flour	½ teaspoon vanilla extract
¾ teaspoon baking powder	Cooking oil spray
Dash sea salt	120 g fresh blueberries
120 ml semi-skimmed milk	60 g granola
2 tablespoons pure maple syrup	

1. In a medium bowl, whisk the flour, baking powder, and salt. Add the milk, maple syrup, and vanilla and gently whisk, just until thoroughly combined. 2. Preheat the unit by selecting BAKE, setting the temperature to 180ºC, and setting the time to 3 minutes. Select START/STOP to begin. 3. Spray a 6-by-2-inch round baking pan with cooking oil and pour the batter into the pan. Top evenly with the blueberries and granola. 4. Once the unit is preheated, place the pan into the basket. 5. Select BAKE, set the temperature to 180ºC, and set the time to 15 minutes. Select START/STOP to begin. 6. When the cooking is complete, the cobbler should be nicely browned and a knife inserted into the middle should come out clean. Enjoy plain or topped with a little vanilla yoghurt.

Oat Bran Muffins

160 g oat bran	1 egg
60 g flour	2 tablespoons rapeseed oil
45 g soft brown sugar	120 g chopped dates, raisins, or
1 teaspoon baking powder	dried cranberries
½ teaspoon baking soda	24 paper muffin cases
⅛ teaspoon salt	Cooking spray
120 ml buttermilk	

1. Preheat the air fryer to 170ºC. 2. In a large bowl, combine the oat bran, flour, soft brown sugar, baking powder, baking soda, and salt. 3. In a small bowl, beat together the buttermilk, egg, and oil. 4. Pour buttermilk mixture into bowl with dry ingredients and stir just until moistened. Do not beat. 5. Gently stir in dried fruit. 6. Use triple baking cups to help muffins hold shape during baking. Spray them with cooking spray, place 4 sets of cups in air fryer basket at a time, and fill each one ¾ full of batter. 7. Cook for 10 to 12 minutes, until top springs back when lightly touched and toothpick inserted in center comes out clean. 8. Repeat for remaining muffins.

Strawberry Toast

4 slices bread, ½-inch thick	235 g sliced strawberries
Butter-flavoured cooking spray	1 teaspoon sugar

1. Spray one side of each bread slice with butter-flavoured cooking spray. Lay slices sprayed side down. 2. Divide the strawberries among the bread slices. 3. Sprinkle evenly with the sugar and place in one of the air fryer baskets in a single layer. 4. Air fry at 200ºC for 8 minutes. The bottom should look brown and crisp and the top should look glazed.

Homemade Cherry Breakfast Tarts

Tarts:	Frosting:
2 refrigerated piecrusts	120 ml vanilla yoghurt
80 g cherry preserves	30 g soft cheese
1 teaspoon cornflour	1 teaspoon stevia
Cooking oil	Rainbow sprinkles

Make the Tarts 1. Place the piecrusts on a flat surface. Using a knife or pizza cutter, cut each piecrust into 3 rectangles, for 6 total. (I discard the unused dough left from slicing the edges.) 2. In a small bowl, combine the preserves and cornflour. Mix well. 3. Scoop 1 tablespoon of the preserves mixture onto the top half of each piece of piecrust. 4. Fold the bottom of each piece up to close the tart. Using the back of a fork, press along the edges of each tart to seal. 5. Spray the breakfast tarts with cooking oil and place them in the air fryer. I do not recommend stacking the breakfast tarts. They will stick together if stacked. You may need to prepare them in two batches. Bake at 190ºC for 10 minutes. 6. Allow the breakfast tarts to cool fully before removing from the air fryer. 7. If necessary, repeat steps 5 and 6 for the remaining breakfast tarts. Make the Frosting 8. In a small bowl, combine the yoghurt, soft cheese, and stevia. Mix well. 9. Spread the breakfast tarts with frosting and top with sprinkles, and serve.

Drop Biscuits

500 g plain flour	for brushing on the biscuits
1 tablespoon baking powder	(optional)
1 tablespoon sugar (optional)	180 ml buttermilk
1 teaspoon salt	1 to 2 tablespoons oil
6 tablespoons butter, plus more	

1. In a large bowl, whisk the flour, baking powder, sugar (if using), and salt until blended. 2. Add the butter. Using a pastry cutter or 2 forks, work the dough until pea-size balls of the butter-flour mixture appear. Stir in the buttermilk until the mixture is sticky. 3. Preheat the air fryer to 170ºC. Line one of the air fryer baskets with parchment paper and spritz it with oil. 4. Drop the dough by the tablespoonful onto the prepared basket, leaving 1 inch between each, to form 10 biscuits. 5. Bake for 5 minutes. Flip the biscuits and cook for 4 minutes more for a light brown top, or 5 minutes more for a darker biscuit. Brush the tops with melted butter, if desired.

Egg Tarts

⅓ sheet frozen puff pastry,	2 eggs
thawed	¼ teaspoon salt, divided
Cooking oil spray	1 teaspoon minced fresh parsley
120 g grated Cheddar cheese	(optional)

1. Insert the crisper plate into the basket and the basket into the unit. Preheat the unit by selecting BAKE, setting the temperature to 200ºC, and setting the time to 3 minutes. Select START/STOP to begin. 2. Lay the puff pastry sheet on a piece of parchment paper and cut it in half. 3. Once the unit is preheated, spray the crisper plate with cooking oil. Transfer the 2 squares of pastry to the basket, keeping them on the parchment paper. 4. Select BAKE, set the temperature to 200ºC, and set the time to 20 minutes. Select START/STOP to begin. 5. After 10 minutes, use a metal spoon to press down the center of each pastry square to make a well. Divide the cheese equally between the baked pastries. Carefully crack an egg on top of the cheese, and sprinkle each with the salt. Resume cooking for 7 to 10 minutes. 6. When the cooking is complete, the eggs will be cooked through. Sprinkle each with parsley (if using) and serve.

Chapter 2 Desserts

Chapter 2 Desserts

Sweet Potato Donut Holes

Prep time: 10 minutes | Cook time: 4 to 5 minutes per batch | Makes 18 donut holes

65 g All-purpose flour	sweet potatoes
50 g granulated sugar	1 egg, beaten
¼ teaspoon baking soda	2 tablespoons butter, melted
1 teaspoon baking powder	1 teaspoon pure vanilla extract
⅛ teaspoon salt	Coconut, or avocado oil for
125 g cooked & mashed purple	misting or cooking spray

1. Preheat the air fryer to 200ºC. 2. In a large bowl, stir together the flour, sugar, baking soda, baking powder, and salt. 3. In a separate bowl, combine the potatoes, egg, butter, and vanilla and mix well. 4. Add potato mixture to dry ingredients and stir into a soft dough. 5. Shape dough into 1½-inch balls. Mist lightly with oil or cooking spray. 6. Place them half in zone 1, the remaining in zone 2. In zone 1, select Air Fry button, set the time to 4 to 5 minutes. In zone 2, select Match Cook and then press Start. 7. If necessary, Repeat step 6 to cook remaining donut holes.

Chickpea Brownies

Prep time: 10 minutes | Cook time: 20 minutes | Serves 6

Vegetable oil	cocoa powder
425 g can chickpeas, drained and rinsed	1 tablespoon espresso powder (optional)
4 large eggs	1 teaspoon baking powder
80 ml coconut oil, melted	1 teaspoon baking soda
80 ml honey	80 g chocolate chips
3 tablespoons unsweetened	

1. Preheat the air fryer to 160ºC. 2. Generously grease a baking pan with vegetable oil. 3. In a blender or food processor, combine the chickpeas, eggs, coconut oil, honey, cocoa powder, espresso powder (if using), baking powder, and baking soda. Blend or process until smooth. Transfer to the prepared pan and stir in the chocolate chips by hand. 4. Set the pan in the air fryer basket and bake for 20 minutes, or until a toothpick inserted into the center comes out clean. 5. Let cool in the pan on a wire rack for 30 minutes before cutting into squares. 6. Serve immediately.

Dark Brownies

Prep time: 10 minutes | Cook time: 11 to 13 minutes | Serves 4

1 egg	30 g cocoa
85 g granulated sugar	Cooking spray
¼ teaspoon salt	Optional:
½ teaspoon vanilla	Vanilla ice cream
55 g unsalted butter, melted	Caramel sauce
15 g All-purpose flour, plus 2 tablespoons	Whipped cream

1. Beat together egg, sugar, salt, and vanilla until light. 2. Add melted butter and mix well. 3. Stir in flour and cocoa. 4. Spray a baking pan with raised sides lightly with cooking spray. 5. Spread batter in pan and bake at 160ºC for 11 to 13 minutes. Cool and cut into 4 large squares or 16 small brownie bites.

Pears with Honey-Lemon Ricotta

Prep time: 10 minutes | Cook time: 8 minutes | Serves 4

2 large Bartlett pears	125 g full-fat ricotta cheese
3 tablespoons butter, melted	1 tablespoon honey, plus
3 tablespoons brown sugar	additional for drizzling
½ teaspoon ground ginger	1 teaspoon pure almond extract
¼ teaspoon ground cardamom	1 teaspoon pure lemon extract

1. Peel each pear and cut in half, lengthwise. Use a melon baller to scoop out the core. Place the pear halves in a medium bowl, add the melted butter, and toss. Add the brown sugar, ginger, and cardamom; toss to coat. 2. Place the pear halves, cut side down, in one of the air fryer baskets. Set the air fryer to 190ºC cooking for 8 to 10 minutes, or until the pears are lightly browned and tender, but not mushy. 3. Meanwhile, in a medium bowl, combine the ricotta, honey, and almond and lemon extracts. Beat with an electric mixer on medium speed until the mixture is light and fluffy, about 1 minute. 4. To serve, divide the ricotta mixture among four small shallow bowls. Place a pear half, cut side up, on top of the cheese. Drizzle with additional honey and serve.

Cream Cheese Danish

Prep time: 20 minutes | Cook time: 15 minutes |
Serves 6

35 g blanched finely ground almond flour
225 g shredded Mozzarella cheese
140 g full-fat cream cheese, divided

2 large egg yolks
75 g powdered sweetener, divided
2 teaspoons vanilla extract, divided

1. In a large microwave-safe bowl, add almond flour, Mozzarella, and 30 g cream cheese. Mix and then microwave for 1 minute. 2. Stir and add egg yolks to the bowl. Continue stirring until soft dough forms. Add 50 g sweetener to dough and 1 teaspoon vanilla. 3. Cut a piece of baking paper to fit your air fryer basket. Wet your hands with warm water and press out the dough into a ¼-inch-thick rectangle. 4. In a medium bowl, mix remaining cream cheese, remaining sweetener, and vanilla. Place this cream cheese mixture on the right half of the dough rectangle. Fold over the left side of the dough and press to seal. Place them half in zone 1, the remaining in zone 2. In zone 1, select Air Fry button, adjust the temperature to 160ºC, set the time to 15 minutes. In zone 2, select Match Cook and then press Start. After 7 minutes, flip over the Danish. 7. When done, remove the Danish from baking paper and allow to completely cool before cutting.

Lemon Raspberry Muffins

Prep time: 5 minutes | Cook time: 15 minutes |
Serves 6

110 g almond flour
40 g powdered sweetener
1¼ teaspoons baking powder
⅓ teaspoon ground allspice
⅓ teaspoon ground star anise
½ teaspoon grated lemon zest

¼ teaspoon salt
2 eggs
240 ml sour cream
120 ml coconut oil
60 g raspberries

1. Preheat the air fryer to 180ºC. Line a muffin pan with 6 paper cases. 2. In a mixing bowl, mix the almond flour, sweetener, baking powder, allspice, star anise, lemon zest, and salt. 3. In another mixing bowl, beat the eggs, sour cream, and coconut oil until well mixed. Add the egg mixture to the flour mixture and stir to combine. Mix in the raspberries. 4. Scrape the batter into the prepared muffin cups, filling each about three-quarters full. 5. Bake for 15 minutes, or until the tops are golden and a toothpick inserted in the middle comes out clean. 6. Allow the muffins to cool for 10 minutes in the muffin pan before removing and serving.

Pumpkin Cookie with Cream Cheese Frosting

Prep time: 10 minutes | Cook time: 7 minutes |
Serves 6

25 g blanched finely ground almond flour
25 g powdered sweetener, divided
2 tablespoons butter, softened
1 large egg
½ teaspoon unflavoured gelatin
½ teaspoon baking powder
½ teaspoon vanilla extract

½ teaspoon pumpkin pie spice
2 tablespoons pure pumpkin purée
½ teaspoon ground cinnamon, divided
40 g low-carb, sugar-free chocolate chips
85 g full-fat cream cheese, softened

1. In a large bowl, mix almond flour and 25 gsweetener. Stir in butter, egg, and gelatin until combined. 2. Stir in baking powder, vanilla, pumpkin pie spice, pumpkin purée, and ¼ teaspoon cinnamon, then fold in chocolate chips. 3. Pour batter into a round baking pan. Place pan into the air fryer basket. 4. Adjust the temperature to 150ºC and bake for 7 minutes. 5. When fully cooked, the top will be golden brown, and a toothpick inserted in center will come out clean. Let cool at least 20 minutes. 6. To make the frosting: mix cream cheese, remaining ¼ teaspoon cinnamon, and remaining 25 g sweetener in a large bowl. Using an electric mixer, beat until it becomes fluffy. Spread onto the cooled cookie. Garnish with additional cinnamon if desired.

Pecan Butter Cookies

Prep time: 5 minutes | Cook time: 24 minutes |
Makes 12 cookies

125 g chopped pecans
110 g salted butter, melted
30 g coconut flour

150 g granulated sweetener, divided
1 teaspoon vanilla extract

1. In a food processor, blend together pecans, butter, flour, 100 g sweetener, and vanilla 1 minute until a dough forms. 2. Form dough into twelve individual cookie balls, about 1 tablespoon each. 3. Cut three pieces of baking paper to fit air fryer basket. Place four cookies on each ungreased baking paper and place one piece baking paper with cookies into air fryer basket. Adjust air fryer temperature to 160ºC and set the timer for 8 minutes. Repeat cooking with remaining batches. 4. When the timer goes off, allow cookies to cool 5 minutes on a large serving plate until cool enough to handle. While still warm, dust cookies with remaining granulated sweetener. Allow to cool completely, about 15 minutes, before serving.

Spiced Apple Cake

Prep time: 15 minutes | Cook time: 30 minutes |

Serves 6

Vegetable oil	1 tablespoon apple pie spice
2 diced & peeled Gala apples	½ teaspoon ground ginger
1 tablespoon fresh lemon juice	¼ teaspoon ground cardamom
55 g unsalted butter, softened	¼ teaspoon ground nutmeg
50 g granulated sugar	½ teaspoon kosher, or coarse
2 large eggs	sea salt
80 g All-purpose flour	60 ml whole milk
1½ teaspoons baking powder	Icing sugar, for dusting

1. Grease a 0.7-liter Bundt, or tube pan with oil; set aside. 2. In a medium bowl, toss the apples with the lemon juice until well coated; set aside. 3. In a large bowl, combine the butter and sugar. Beat with an electric hand mixer on medium speed until the sugar has dissolved. Add the eggs and beat until fluffy. Add the flour, baking powder, apple pie spice, ginger, cardamom, nutmeg, salt, and milk. Mix until the batter is thick but pourable. 4. Pour the batter into the prepared pan. Top batter evenly with the apple mixture. Place the pan in the air fryer basket. Set the air fryer to 180°C and cook for 30 minutes, or until a toothpick inserted in the center of the cake comes out clean. Close the air fryer and let the cake rest for 10 minutes. Turn the cake out onto a wire rack and cool completely. 5. Right before serving, dust the cake with icing sugar.

Apple Fries

Prep time: 10 minutes | Cook time: 7 minutes |

Serves 8

Coconut, or avocado oil, for spraying	40 g granulated sugar
	1 teaspoon ground cinnamon
55 g All-purpose flour	3 large Gala apples, peeled,
3 large eggs, beaten	cored and cut into wedges
100 g crushed digestive biscuits	240 ml caramel sauce, warmed

1. Preheat the air fryer to 190°C. Line the air fryer basket with baking paper and spray lightly with oil. 2. Place the flour and beaten eggs in separate bowls and set aside. In another bowl, mix together the crushed biscuits, sugar and cinnamon. 3. Working one at a time, coat the apple wedges in the flour, dip in the egg and then dredge in the biscuit mix until evenly coated. 4. Place them half in zone 1, the remaining in zone 2. In zone 1, select Air Fry button, set the time to 5 minutes. In zone 2, select Match Cook and then press Start. Taking care not to overlap, and spray lightly with oil. You may need to work in batches, depending on the size of your air fryer. 5. Flip, spray with oil, and cook for another 2 minutes, or until crunchy and golden brown. 6. Drizzle the caramel sauce over the top and serve.

Almond Butter Cookie Balls

Prep time: 5 minutes | Cook time: 10 minutes |

Makes 10 balls

70 g almond butter	25 g desiccated unsweetened
1 large egg	coconut
1 teaspoon vanilla extract	40 g low-carb, sugar-free
30 g low-carb protein powder	chocolate chips
15 g powdered sweetener	½ teaspoon ground cinnamon

1. In a large bowl, mix almond butter and egg. Add in vanilla, protein powder, and sweetener. 2. Fold in coconut, chocolate chips, and cinnamon. Roll into 1-inch balls. Place balls into a round baking pan and put into one of the air fryer baskets. 3. Adjust the temperature to 160°C and bake for 10 minutes. 4. Allow to cool completely. Store in an airtight container in the refrigerator up to 4 days.

New York Cheesecake

Prep time: 1 hour | Cook time: 37 minutes | Serves 8

65 g almond flour	340 g granulated sweetener
45 g powdered sweetener	3 eggs, at room temperature
55 g unsalted butter, melted	1 tablespoon vanilla essence
565 g full-fat cream cheese	1 teaspoon grated lemon zest
120 ml heavy cream	

1. Coat the sides and bottom of a baking pan with a little flour. 2. In a mixing bowl, combine the almond flour and powdered sweetener. Add the melted butter and mix until your mixture looks like breadcrumbs. 3. Press the mixture into the bottom of the prepared pan to form an even layer. Bake at 160°C for 7 minutes until golden brown. Allow it to cool completely on a wire rack. 4. Meanwhile, in a mixer fitted with the paddle attachment, prepare the filling by mixing the soft cheese, heavy cream, and granulated sweetener; beat until creamy and fluffy. 5. Crack the eggs into the mixing bowl, one at a time; add the vanilla and lemon zest and continue to mix until fully combined. 6. Pour the prepared topping over the cooled crust and spread evenly. 7. Bake in the preheated air fryer at 160°C for 25 to 30 minutes; leave it in the air fryer to keep warm for another 30 minutes. 8. Cover your cheesecake with plastic wrap. Place in your refrigerator and allow it to cool at least 6 hours or overnight. Serve well chilled.

Chocolate Chip Pecan Biscotti

Prep time: 15 minutes | Cook time: 20 to 22 minutes | Serves 10

70 g finely ground blanched almond flour

¾ teaspoon baking powder

½ teaspoon xanthan gum

¼ teaspoon sea salt

3 tablespoons unsalted butter, at room temperature

35 g powdered sweetener

1 large egg, beaten

1 teaspoon pure vanilla extract

50 g chopped pecans

40 g organic chocolate chips,

Melted organic chocolate chips and chopped pecans, for topping (optional)

1. In a large bowl, combine the almond flour, baking powder, xanthan gum, and salt. 2. Line a cake pan that fits inside your air fryer with baking paper. 3. In the bowl of a stand mixer, beat together the butter and powdered sweetener. Add the beaten egg and vanilla and beat for about 3 minutes. 4. Add the almond flour mixture to the butter and egg mixture; beat until just combined. 5. Stir in the pecans and chocolate chips. 6. Transfer the dough to the prepared pan and press it into the bottom. 7. Set the air fryer to 160ºC and bake for 12 minutes. Remove from the air fryer and let cool for 15 minutes. Using a sharp knife, cut the cookie into thin strips, then return the strips to the cake pan with the bottom sides facing up. 8. Set the air fryer to 150ºC. Bake for 8 to 10 minutes. 9. Remove from the air fryer and let cool completely on a wire rack. If desired, dip one side of each biscotti piece into melted chocolate chips, and top with chopped pecans.

S'mores

Prep time: 5 minutes | Cook time: 30 seconds | Makes 8 s'mores

Coconut, or avocado oil, for spraying

8 digestive biscuits

2 (45 g) chocolate bars

4 large marshmallows

1. Line one of the air fryer baskets with baking paper and spray lightly with oil. 2. Place 4 biscuits into the prepared basket. 3. Break the chocolate bars in half, and place 1/2 on top of each biscuit. Top with 1 marshmallow. 4. Air fry at 190ºC for 30 seconds, or until the marshmallows are puffed, golden brown and slightly melted. 5. Top with the remaining biscuits and serve.

Cream-Filled Sponge Cakes

Prep time: 10 minutes | Cook time: 10 minutes | Makes 4 cakes

Coconut, or avocado oil, for spraying

1 tube croissant dough

4 Swiss rolls

1 tablespoon icing sugar

1. Line one of the air fryer baskets with baking paper, and spray lightly with oil. 2. Unroll the dough into a single flat layer and cut it into 4 equal pieces. 3. Place 1 sponge cake in the center of each piece of dough. Wrap the dough around the cake, pinching the ends to seal. 4. Place the wrapped cakes in the prepared basket, and spray lightly with oil. 5. Bake at 90ºC for 5 minutes, flip, spray with oil, and cook for another 5 minutes, or until golden brown. 6. Dust with the icing sugar and serve.

Chapter 3 Beef, Pork, and Lamb

Chapter 3 Beef, Pork, and Lamb

Greek-Style Meatloaf & Spice-Rubbed Pork Loin

Prep time: 10 minutes | Cook time: 25 minutes

Greek-Style Meatloaf | Serves 6:
450 g lean beef mince
2 eggs
2 plum tomatoes, diced
½ brown onion, diced
60 g whole wheat bread crumbs
1 teaspoon garlic powder
1 teaspoon dried oregano
1 teaspoon dried thyme
1 teaspoon salt
1 teaspoon black pepper
60 g mozzarella cheese, shredded

1 tablespoon olive oil
Fresh chopped parsley, for garnish
Spice-Rubbed Pork Loin | Serves 6:
1 teaspoon paprika
½ teaspoon ground cumin
½ teaspoon chili powder
½ teaspoon garlic powder
2 tablespoons coconut oil
1 (680 g) boneless pork loin
½ teaspoon salt
¼ teaspoon ground black pepper

Prepare for Greek-Style Meatloaf:
1. Preheat the oven to 190ºC.
2. In a large bowl, mix together the beef, eggs, tomatoes, onion, bread crumbs, garlic powder, oregano, thyme, salt, pepper, and cheese.
3. Form into a loaf, flattening to 1-inch thick. 4. Brush the top with olive oil, then place the meatloaf into zone 1.
Prepare for Spice-Rubbed Pork Loin:
1. In a small bowl, mix paprika, cumin, chili powder, and garlic powder.
2. Drizzle coconut oil over pork. Sprinkle pork loin with salt and pepper, then rub spice mixture evenly on all sides.
3. Place pork loin into ungreased zone 2.
Cook:
1. In zone 1, adjust the air fryer temperature to 190ºC and air fry for 25 minutes.
2. In zone 2, adjust the air fryer temperature to 200ºC and air fry for 20 minutes.
3. Press SYNC, then press Start.
4. For zone 1, remove from the air fryer and allow to rest for 5 minutes, before slicing and serving with a sprinkle of parsley.
5. For zone 2, turning pork halfway through cooking. Pork loin will be browned and have an internal temperature of at least 64ºC when done. Serve warm.

Deconstructed Chicago Dogs

Prep time: 10 minutes | Cook time: 7 minutes | Serves 4

4 hot dogs
2 large dill pickles
60 g diced onions
1 tomato, cut into ½-inch dice
4 pickled or brined jalapeno

peppers, diced
For Garnish (Optional):
Wholegrain or Dijon mustard
Celery salt
Poppy seeds

1. Spray one of the air fryer baskets with avocado oil. Preheat the air fryer to 200ºC. 2. Place the hot dogs in one of the air fryer baskets and air fry for 5 to 7 minutes, until hot and slightly crispy. 3. While the hot dogs cook, quarter one of the dill pickles lengthwise, so that you have 4 pickle spears. Finely dice the other pickle. 4. When the hot dogs are done, transfer them to a serving platter and arrange them in a row, alternating with the pickle spears. Top with the diced pickles, onions, tomato, and jalapeno peppers. Drizzle mustard on top and garnish with celery salt and poppy seeds, if desired. 5. Best served fresh. Store leftover hot dogs in an airtight container in the refrigerator for up to 3 days. Reheat in a preheated 200ºC air fryer for 2 minutes, or until warmed through.

Super Bacon with Meat

Prep time: 5 minutes | Cook time: 1 hour | Serves 4

30 slices thick-cut bacon
110 g Cheddar cheese, shredded
340 g steak

280 g pork sausage meat
Salt and ground black pepper, to taste

1. Preheat the air fryer to 200ºC. 2. Lay out 30 slices of bacon in a woven pattern and bake for 20 minutes until crisp. Put the cheese in the center of the bacon. 3. Combine the steak and sausage to form a meaty mixture. 4. Lay out the meat in a rectangle of similar size to the bacon strips. Season with salt and pepper. 5. Roll the meat into a tight roll and refrigerate. 6. Preheat the air fryer to 200ºC. 7. Make a 7×7 bacon weave and roll the bacon weave over the meat, diagonally. 8. Bake for 60 minutes or until the internal temperature reaches at least 74ºC. 9. Let rest for 5 minutes before serving.

Pork Loin Roast

Prep time: 30 minutes | Cook time: 55 minutes |
Serves 6

680 g boneless pork loin joint, washed	¾ teaspoon sea salt flakes
1 teaspoon mustard seeds	1 teaspoon red pepper flakes, crushed
1 teaspoon garlic powder	2 dried sprigs thyme, crushed
1 teaspoon porcini powder	2 tablespoons lime juice
1 teaspoon onion granules	

1. Firstly, score the meat using a small knife; make sure to not cut too deep. 2. In a small-sized mixing dish, combine all seasonings in the order listed above; mix to combine well. 3. Massage the spice mix into the pork meat to evenly distribute. Drizzle with lemon juice. 4. Set the air fryer to 180ºC. Place the pork in the air fryer basket; roast for 25 to 30 minutes. Pause the machine, check for doneness and cook for 25 minutes more.

Pork and Tricolor Vegetables Kebabs

Prep time: 1 hour 20 minutes | Cook time: 8 minutes per batch | Serves 4

For the Pork:	1 courgette, cut in cubes
450 g pork steak, cut in cubes	1 butternut squash, deseeded and cut in cubes
1 tablespoon white wine vinegar	1 red pepper, cut in cubes
3 tablespoons steak sauce or brown sauce	1 green pepper, cut in cubes
60 ml soy sauce	Salt and ground black pepper, to taste
1 teaspoon powdered chili	Cooking spray
1 teaspoon red chili flakes	Special Equipment:
2 teaspoons smoked paprika	4 bamboo skewers, soaked in water for at least 30 minutes
1 teaspoon garlic salt	
For the Vegetable:	

1. Combine the ingredients for the pork in a large bowl. Press the pork to dunk in the marinade. Wrap the bowl in plastic and refrigerate for at least an hour. 2. Preheat the air fryer to 190ºC and spritz with cooking spray. 3. Remove the pork from the marinade and run the skewers through the pork and vegetables alternatively. Sprinkle with salt and pepper to taste. 4. Arrange the skewers in the preheated air fryer and spritz with cooking spray. Air fry for 8 minutes or until the pork is browned and the vegetables are lightly charred and tender. Flip the skewers halfway through. You may need to work in batches to avoid overcrowding. 5. Serve immediately.

Roast Beef with Horseradish Cream

Prep time: 5 minutes | Cook time: 35 to 45 minutes |
Serves 6

900 g beef roasting joint	80 ml double cream
1 tablespoon salt	80 ml sour cream
2 teaspoons garlic powder	80 g grated horseradish
1 teaspoon freshly ground black pepper	2 teaspoons fresh lemon juice
1 teaspoon dried thyme	Salt and freshly ground black pepper, to taste
Horseradish Cream:	

1. Preheat the air fryer to 200ºC. 2. Season the beef with the salt, garlic powder, black pepper, and thyme. Place the beef fat-side down in the basket of the air fryer and lightly coat with olive oil. Pausing halfway through the cooking time to turn the meat, air fry for 35 to 45 minutes, until a thermometer inserted into the thickest part indicates the desired doneness, 52ºC (rare) to 64ºC (medium). Let the beef rest for 10 minutes before slicing. 3. To make the horseradish cream: In a small bowl, combine the double cream, sour cream, horseradish, and lemon juice. Whisk until thoroughly combined. Season to taste with salt and freshly ground black pepper. Serve alongside the beef.

Beef Burgers with Mushroom

Prep time: 10 minutes | Cook time: 21 to 23 minutes | Serves 4

450 g beef mince, formed into 4 patties	230 g mushrooms, sliced
Sea salt and freshly ground black pepper, to taste	1 tablespoon avocado oil
235 g thinly sliced onion	60 g Gruyère cheese, shredded (about 120 ml)

1. Season the patties on both sides with salt and pepper. 2. Set the air fryer to 190ºC. Place the patties in the basket and cook for 3 minutes. Flip and cook for another 2 minutes. Remove the burgers and set aside. 3. Place the onion and mushrooms in a medium bowl. Add the avocado oil and salt and pepper to taste; toss well. 4. Place the onion and mushrooms in one of the air fryer baskets. Cook for 15 minutes, stirring occasionally. 5. Spoon the onions and mushrooms over the patties. Top with the cheese. Place the patties back in one of the air fryer baskets and cook for another 1 to 3 minutes, until the cheese melts and an instant-read thermometer reads 72ºC. Remove and let rest. The temperature will rise to 74ºC, yielding a perfect medium-well burger.

Sausage and Courgette Lasagna

Prep time: 25 minutes | Cook time: 56 minutes | Serves 4

1 courgette
Avocado oil spray
170 g hot Italian-seasoned
sausage, casings removed
60 g mushrooms, stemmed and
sliced
1 teaspoon minced garlic
235 ml keto-friendly marinara
sauce

180 g ricotta cheese
235 g shredded gruyere cheese,
divided
120 g finely grated Parmesan
cheese
Sea salt and freshly ground
black pepper, to taste
Fresh basil, for garnish

1. Cut the courgette into long thin slices using a mandoline slicer or sharp knife. Spray both sides of the slices with oil. 2. Place the slices in a single layer in one of the air fryer baskets, working in batches if necessary. Set the air fryer to 160ºC and air fry for 4 to 6 minutes, until most of the moisture has been released from the courgette. 3. Place a large skillet over medium-high heat. Crumble the sausage into the hot skillet and cook for 6 minutes, breaking apart the meat with the back of a spoon. Remove the sausage from the skillet, leaving any fats that remain. Add the mushrooms to the skillet and cook for 10 minutes, until the liquid nearly evaporates. Add the garlic and cook for 1 minute more. Stir in the marinara and cook for 2 more minutes. 4. In a medium bowl, combine the ricotta cheese, 120 ml of gruyere cheese, Parmesan cheese, and salt and pepper to taste. 5. Spread 60 ml of the meat sauce in the bottom of a deep pan (or other pan that fits inside your air fryer). Top with half of the courgette slices. Add half of the cheese mixture. Top the cheese with half of the remaining meat sauce. Layer the remaining courgette over the meat sauce and top with the remaining cheese mixture. Top the lasagna with the remaining 120 ml of fontina cheese. 6. Cover the lasagna with aluminum foil or parchment paper and place it in the air fryer. Bake for 25 minutes. Remove the foil and cook for 8 to 10 minutes more. 7. Allow the lasagna to rest for 15 minutes before cutting and serving. Garnish with basil.

Fruited Ham & Kheema Meatloaf

Prep time: 25 minutes | Cook time: 15 minutes

Fruited Ham | Serves 4:
235 ml orange marmalade
48 g packed light brown sugar
¼ teaspoon ground cloves
½ teaspoon mustard powder
1 to 2 tablespoons oil
450 g cooked ham, cut into
1-inch cubes
120 g canned mandarin oranges,

drained and chopped
Kheema Meatloaf | Serves 4:
450 g 85% lean beef mince
2 large eggs, lightly beaten
235 g diced brown onion
60 g chopped fresh coriander
1 tablespoon minced fresh
ginger
1 tablespoon minced garlic

2 teaspoons garam masala
1 teaspoon coarse or flaky salt
1 teaspoon ground turmeric

1 teaspoon cayenne pepper
½ teaspoon ground cinnamon
⅛ teaspoon ground cardamom

Prepare for Fruited Ham:
1. In a small bowl, stir together the orange marmalade, brown sugar, cloves, and mustard powder until blended. Set aside.
2. Preheat zone 1 to 160ºC. Spritz a baking tray with oil.
3. Place the ham cubes in the prepared pan. Pour the marmalade sauce over the ham to glaze it.
Prepare for Kheema Meatloaf:
1. In a large bowl, gently mix the beef mince, eggs, onion, coriander, ginger, garlic, garam masala, salt, turmeric, cayenne, cinnamon, and cardamom until thoroughly combined.
2. Place the seasoned meat in a baking tray. Place the pan in zone 2. Cook:
1. In zone 1, adjust the air fryer temperature to 160ºC and air fry for 4 minutes.
2. In zone 2, adjust the air fryer temperature to 180ºC and air fry for 15 minutes.
3. Press SYNC, then press Start.
4. For zone 1, stir and cook for 2 minutes more. Add the mandarin oranges and cook for 2 to 4 minutes more until the sauce begins to thicken and the ham is tender.
5. For zone 2, use a meat thermometer to ensure the meat loaf has reached an internal temperature of 72ºC (medium). Drain the fat and liquid from the pan and let stand for 5 minutes before slicing. Slice and serve hot.

Ham with Sweet Potatoes

Prep time: 20 minutes | Cook time: 15 to 17 minutes | Serves 4

235 g freshly squeezed orange
juice
96 g packed light brown sugar
1 tablespoon Dijon mustard
½ teaspoon salt
½ teaspoon freshly ground

black pepper
3 sweet potatoes, cut into small
wedges
2 gammon steaks (230 g each),
halved
1 to 2 tablespoons oil

1. In a large bowl, whisk the orange juice, brown sugar, Dijon, salt, and pepper until blended. Toss the sweet potato wedges with the brown sugar mixture. 2. Preheat the air fryer to 200ºC. Line one of the air fryer baskets with parchment paper and spritz with oil. 3. Place the sweet potato wedges on the parchment. 4. Cook for 10 minutes. 5. Place gammon steaks on top of the sweet potatoes and brush everything with more of the orange juice mixture. 6. Cook for 3 minutes. Flip the gammon and cook or 2 to 4 minutes more until the sweet potatoes are soft and the glaze has thickened. Cut the gammon steaks in half to serve.

Rack of Lamb with Pistachio Crust

Prep time: 10 minutes | Cook time: 19 minutes |
Serves 2

120 g finely chopped pistachios	Salt and freshly ground black
3 tablespoons panko bread	pepper, to taste
crumbs	1 tablespoon olive oil
1 teaspoon chopped fresh	1 rack of lamb, bones trimmed
rosemary	of fat and frenched
2 teaspoons chopped fresh	1 tablespoon Dijon mustard
oregano	

1. Preheat the air fryer to 190°C. 2. Combine the pistachios, bread crumbs, rosemary, oregano, salt and pepper in a small bowl. (This is a good job for your food processor if you have one.) Drizzle in the olive oil and stir to combine. 3. Season the rack of lamb with salt and pepper on all sides and transfer it to one of the air fryer baskets with the fat side facing up. Air fry the lamb for 12 minutes. Remove the lamb from the air fryer and brush the fat side of the lamb rack with the Dijon mustard. Coat the rack with the pistachio mixture, pressing the bread crumbs onto the lamb with your hands and rolling the bottom of the rack in any of the crumbs that fall off. 4. Return the rack of lamb to the air fryer and air fry for another 3 to 7 minutes or until an instant read thermometer reads 60°C for medium. Add or subtract a couple of minutes for lamb that is more or less well cooked. (Your time will vary depending on how big the rack of lamb is.) 5. Let the lamb rest for at least 5 minutes. Then, slice into chops and serve.

Meat and Rice Stuffed Peppers

Prep time: 20 minutes | Cook time: 18 minutes |
Serves 4

340 g lean beef mince	½ teaspoon dried basil
110 g lean pork mince	120 g cooked brown rice
60 g onion, minced	½ teaspoon garlic powder
1 (425 g) can finely-chopped	½ teaspoon oregano
tomatoes	½ teaspoon salt
1 teaspoon Worcestershire	2 small peppers, cut in half,
sauce	stems removed, deseeded
1 teaspoon barbecue seasoning	Cooking spray
1 teaspoon honey	

1. Preheat the air fryer to 180°C and spritz a baking tray with cooking spray. 2. Arrange the beef, pork, and onion in the baking tray and bake in the preheated air fryer for 8 minutes. Break the ground meat into chunks halfway through the cooking. 3. Meanwhile, combine the tomatoes, Worcestershire sauce, barbecue seasoning, honey, and basil in a saucepan. Stir to mix well. 4. Transfer the cooked meat mixture to a large bowl and add the cooked rice, garlic powder, oregano, salt, and 60 ml of the tomato mixture. Stir to mix well. 5. Stuff the pepper halves with the mixture, then arrange the pepper halves in the air fryer and air fry for 10 minutes or until the peppers are lightly charred. 6. Serve the stuffed peppers with the remaining tomato sauce on top.

Garlic Butter Steak Bites & Beef Fillet with Thyme and Parsley

Prep time: 10 minutes | Cook time: 16 minutes

Garlic Butter Steak Bites		¼ teaspoon freshly ground
Serves 3:	black pepper
Oil, for spraying	Beef Fillet with Thyme and
450 g boneless steak, cut into	Parsley	Serves 4:
1-inch pieces	1 tablespoon melted butter
2 tablespoons olive oil	¼ dried thyme
1 teaspoon Worcestershire	1 teaspoon garlic salt
sauce	¼ teaspoon dried parsley
½ teaspoon granulated garlic	450 g beef fillet
½ teaspoon salt	

Prepare for Garlic Butter Steak Bites:
1. Preheat the air fryer to 200°C. Line zone 1 with parchment and spray lightly with oil.
2. In a medium bowl, combine the steak, olive oil, Worcestershire sauce, garlic, salt, and black pepper and toss until evenly coated.
3. Place the steak in a single layer in the prepared basket. You may have to work in batches, depending on the size of your air fryer.
Prepare for Beef Fillet with Thyme and Parsley:
1. Preheat the air fryer to 200°C.
2. In a bowl, combine the melted butter, thyme, garlic salt, and parsley.
3. Cut the beef fillet into slices and generously apply the seasoned butter using a brush. Transfer to zone 2.
Cook:
1. In zone 1, adjust the air fryer temperature to 200°C and air fry for 10 to 16 minutes.
2. In zone 2, adjust the air fryer temperature to 200°C and air fry for 15 minutes.
3. Press SYNC, then press Start.
4. For zone 1, flipping every 3 to 4 minutes. The total cooking time will depend on the thickness of the meat and your preferred doneness. If you want it well done, it may take up to 5 additional minutes.

Beef Whirls

Prep time: 30 minutes | Cook time: 18 minutes |
Serves 6

3 minute steaks (170 g each)
1 (450 g) bottle Italian dressing
120 g Italian-style bread crumbs
(or plain bread crumbs with
Italian seasoning to taste)
120 g grated Parmesan cheese

1 teaspoon dried basil
1 teaspoon dried oregano
1 teaspoon dried parsley
60 ml beef stock
1 to 2 tablespoons oil

1. In a large resealable bag, combine the steaks and Italian dressing. Seal the bag and refrigerate to marinate for 2 hours. 2. In a medium bowl, whisk the bread crumbs, cheese, basil, oregano, and parsley until blended. Stir in the beef stock. 3. Place the steaks on a cutting board and cut each in half so you have 6 equal pieces. Sprinkle with the bread crumb mixture. Roll up the steaks, jelly roll-style, and secure with toothpicks. 4. Preheat the air fryer to 200ºC. 5. Place them half in zone 1, the remaining in zone 2. In zone 1, select Air Fry button, set the time to 5 minutes. In zone 2, select Match Cook and then press Start. 6. Flip the roll-ups and spritz with oil. Cook for 4 minutes more until the internal temperature reaches 64ºC. Repeat with the remaining roll-ups. Let rest for 5 to 10 minutes before serving.

Sausage and Pork Meatballs

Prep time: 15 minutes | Cook time: 8 to 12 minutes |
Serves 8

1 large egg
1 teaspoon gelatin
450 g pork mince
230 g Italian-seasoned sausage,
casings removed, crumbled
80 g Parmesan cheese
60 g finely diced onion
1 tablespoon tomato paste

1 teaspoon minced garlic
1 teaspoon dried oregano
¼ teaspoon red pepper flakes
Sea salt and freshly ground
black pepper, to taste
Keto-friendly marinara sauce,
for serving

1. Beat the egg in a small bowl and sprinkle with the gelatin. Allow to sit for 5 minutes. 2. In a large bowl, combine the pork mince, sausage, Parmesan, onion, tomato paste, garlic, oregano, and red pepper flakes. Season with salt and black pepper. 3. Stir the gelatin mixture, then add it to the other ingredients and, using clean hands, mix to ensure that everything is well combined. Form into 1½-inch round meatballs. 4. Set the air fryer to 200ºC. Place them half in zone 1, the remaining in zone 2. In zone 1, select Air Fry button, set the time to 5 minutes. In zone 2, select Match Cook and then press Start. Flip and cook for 3 to 7 minutes more, or until an instant-read thermometer reads 72ºC.

Green Pepper Cheeseburgers

Prep time: 5 minutes | Cook time: 30 minutes |
Serves 4

2 green peppers
680 g 85% lean beef mince
1 clove garlic, minced
1 teaspoon salt
½ teaspoon freshly ground

black pepper
4 slices Cheddar cheese (about
85 g)
4 large lettuce leaves

1. Preheat the air fryer to 200ºC. 2. Arrange the peppers in the basket of the air fryer. Pausing halfway through the cooking time to turn the peppers, air fry for 20 minutes, or until they are softened and beginning to char. Transfer the peppers to a large bowl and cover with a plate. When cool enough to handle, peel off the skin, remove the seeds and stems, and slice into strips. Set aside. 3. Meanwhile, in a large bowl, combine the beef with the garlic, salt, and pepper. Shape the beef into 4 patties. 4. Lower the heat on the air fryer to 180ºC. Arrange the burgers in a single layer in the basket of the air fryer. Pausing halfway through the cooking time to turn the burgers, air fry for 10 minutes, or until a thermometer inserted into the thickest part registers 72ºC. 5. Top the burgers with the cheese slices and continue baking for a minute or two, just until the cheese has melted. Serve the burgers on a lettuce leaf topped with the roasted peppers.

Jalapeño Popper Pork Chops

Prep time: 15 minutes | Cook time: 6 to 8 minutes |
Serves 4

800 g bone-in, loin pork chops
Sea salt and freshly ground
black pepper, to taste
170 g cream cheese, at room
temperature

110 g sliced bacon, cooked and
crumbled
110 g Cheddar cheese, shredded
1 jalapeño, seeded and diced
1 teaspoon garlic powder

1. Cut a pocket into each pork chop, lengthwise along the side, making sure not to cut it all the way through. Season the outside of the chops with salt and pepper. 2. In a small bowl, combine the cream cheese, bacon, Cheddar cheese, jalapeño, and garlic powder. Divide this mixture among the pork chops, stuffing it into the pocket of each chop. 3. Set the air fryer to 200ºC. Place the pork chops in one of the air fryer baskets in a single layer, working in batches if necessary. Air fry for 3 minutes. Flip the chops and cook for 3 to 5 minutes more, until an instant-read thermometer reads 64ºC. 4. Allow the chops to rest for 5 minutes, then serve warm.

Sesame Beef Lettuce Tacos

Prep time: 30 minutes | Cook time: 8 to 10 minutes | Serves 4

60 ml soy sauce or tamari	450 g bavette or skirt steak
60 ml avocado oil	8 butterhead lettuce leaves
2 tablespoons cooking sherry	2 spring onions, sliced
1 tablespoon granulated sweetener	1 tablespoon toasted sesame seeds
1 tablespoon ground cumin	Hot sauce, for serving
1 teaspoon minced garlic	Lime wedges, for serving
Sea salt and freshly ground black pepper, to taste	Flaky sea salt (optional)

1. In a small bowl, whisk together the soy sauce, avocado oil, cooking sherry, sweetener, cumin, garlic, and salt and pepper to taste. 2. Place the steak in a shallow dish. Pour the marinade over the beef. Cover the dish with plastic wrap and let it marinate in the refrigerator for at least 2 hours or overnight. 3. Remove the flank steak from the dish and discard the marinade. 4. Set the air fryer to 200ºC. Place the steak in one of the air fryer baskets and air fry for 4 to 6 minutes. Flip the steak and cook for 4 minutes more, until an instant-read thermometer reads 49ºC at the thickest part (or cook it to your desired doneness). Allow the steak to rest for 10 minutes, then slice it thinly against the grain. 5. Stack 2 lettuce leaves on top of each other and add some sliced meat. Top with spring onions and sesame seeds. Drizzle with hot sauce and lime juice, and finish with a little flaky salt (if using). Repeat with the remaining lettuce leaves and fillings.

Asian Glazed Meatballs

Prep time: 15 minutes | Cook time: 10 minutes per batch | Serves 4 to 6

1 large shallot, finely chopped	taste
2 cloves garlic, minced	450 g beef mince
1 tablespoon grated fresh ginger	230 g pork mince
2 teaspoons fresh thyme, finely chopped	3 egg yolks
355 g brown mushrooms, very finely chopped (a food processor works well here)	235 ml Thai sweet chili sauce (spring roll sauce)
	60 g toasted sesame seeds
2 tablespoons soy sauce	2 spring onionspring onions, sliced
Freshly ground black pepper, to	

1. Combine the shallot, garlic, ginger, thyme, mushrooms, soy sauce, freshly ground black pepper, beef and pork mince, and egg yolks in a bowl and mix the ingredients together. Gently shape the mixture into 24 balls, about the size of a golf ball. 2. Preheat the air fryer to 190ºC. 3. Working in batches, air fry the meatballs for 8 minutes, turning the meatballs over halfway through the cooking time. Drizzle some of the Thai sweet chili sauce on top of each meatball and return the basket to the air fryer, air frying for another 2 minutes. Reserve the remaining Thai sweet chili sauce for serving. 4. As soon as the meatballs are done, sprinkle with toasted sesame seeds and transfer them to a serving platter. Scatter the spring onionspring onions around and serve warm.

Pork Tenderloin with Avocado Lime Sauce

Prep time: 30 minutes | Cook time: 15 minutes | Serves 4

Marinade:	120 ml full-fat sour cream (or coconut cream for dairy-free)
120 ml lime juice	
Grated zest of 1 lime	Grated zest of 1 lime
2 teaspoons stevia glycerite, or ¼ teaspoon liquid stevia	Juice of 1 lime
3 cloves garlic, minced	2 cloves garlic, roughly chopped
1½ teaspoons fine sea salt	½ teaspoon fine sea salt
1 teaspoon chili powder, or more for more heat	¼ teaspoon ground black pepper
1 teaspoon smoked paprika	Chopped fresh coriander leaves, for garnish
450 g pork tenderloin	
Avocado Lime Sauce:	Lime slices, for serving
1 medium-sized ripe avocado, roughly chopped	Pico de gallo or salsa, for serving

1. In a medium-sized casserole dish, stir together all the marinade ingredients until well combined. Add the tenderloin and coat it well in the marinade. Cover and place in the fridge to marinate for 2 hours or overnight. 2. Spray one of the air fryer baskets with avocado oil. Preheat the air fryer to 200ºC. 3. Remove the pork from the marinade and place it in one of the air fryer baskets. Air fry for 13 to 15 minutes, until the internal temperature of the pork is 64ºC, flipping after 7 minutes. Remove the pork from the air fryer and place it on a cutting board. Allow it to rest for 8 to 10 minutes, then cut it into ½-inch-thick slices. 4. While the pork cooks, make the avocado lime sauce: Place all the sauce ingredients in a food processor and purée until smooth. Taste and adjust the seasoning to your liking. 5. Place the pork slices on a serving platter and spoon the avocado lime sauce on top. Garnish with coriander leaves and serve with lime slices and pico de gallo. 6. Store leftovers in an airtight container in the fridge for up to 4 days. Reheat in a preheated 200ºC air fryer for 5 minutes, or until heated through.

Cheese Crusted Chops & Parmesan-Crusted Pork Chops

Prep time: 15 minutes | Cook time: 12 minutes | Serves 4 to 6

Cheese Crusted Chops | Serves4 to 6:
¼ teaspoon pepper
½ teaspoons salt
4 to 6 thick boneless pork chops
235 g pork scratching crumbs
¼ teaspoon chili powder
½ teaspoons onion granules
1 teaspoon smoked paprika
2 beaten eggs

3 tablespoons grated Parmesan cheese
Cooking spray
Parmesan-Crusted Pork Chops | Serves 4:
1 large egg
120 g grated Parmesan cheese
4 (110 g) boneless pork chops
½ teaspoon salt
¼ teaspoon ground black pepper

Prepare for Cheese Crusted Chops:
1. Preheat the air fryer to 210°C.
2. Rub the pepper and salt on both sides of pork chops.
3. In a food processor, pulse pork scratchings into crumbs. Mix crumbs with chili powder, onion granules, and paprika in a bowl.
4. Beat eggs in another bowl.
5. Dip pork chops into eggs then into pork scratchings crumb mixture.
6. Spritz zone 1 basket with cooking spray and add pork chops to the basket.
Prepare for Parmesan-Crusted Pork Chops:
1. Whisk egg in a medium bowl and place Parmesan in a separate medium bowl.
2. Sprinkle pork chops on both sides with salt and pepper. Dip each pork chop into egg, then press both sides into Parmesan.
3. Place pork chops into ungreased zone 2.
Cook:
1. In zone 1, adjust the air fryer temperature to 210°C and air fry for 12 minutes.
2. In zone 2, adjust the air fryer temperature to 200°C and air fry for 12 minutes.
3. Press SYNC, then press Start.
4. For zone 1, serve garnished with the Parmesan cheese.
5. For zone 2, turning chops halfway through cooking. Pork chops will be golden and have an internal temperature of at least 64°C when done. Serve warm.

Chapter 4 Poultry

Chapter 4 Poultry

Crisp Paprika Chicken Drumsticks & Ginger Turmeric Chicken Thighs

Prep time: 10 minutes | Cook time: 25 minutes

Crisp Paprika Chicken
Drumsticks | Serves 2:
2 teaspoons paprika
1 teaspoon packed brown sugar
1 teaspoon garlic powder
½ teaspoon dry mustard
½ teaspoon salt
Pinch pepper
4 (140 g) chicken drumsticks,
trimmed
1 teaspoon vegetable oil
1 scallion, green part only,
sliced thin on bias

Ginger Turmeric Chicken
Thighs | Serves 4:
4 (115 g) boneless, skin-on
chicken thighs
2 tablespoons coconut oil,
melted
½ teaspoon ground turmeric
½ teaspoon salt
½ teaspoon garlic powder
½ teaspoon ground ginger
¼ teaspoon ground black
pepper

Prepare for Crisp Paprika Chicken Drumsticks:
1. Preheat the air fryer to 200ºC.
2. Combine paprika, sugar, garlic powder, mustard, salt, and pepper in a bowl. Pat drumsticks dry with paper towels. Using metal skewer, poke 10 to 15 holes in skin of each drumstick. Rub with oil and sprinkle evenly with spice mixture. 3. Arrange drumsticks in zone 1, spaced evenly apart, alternating ends.
Prepare for Ginger Turmeric Chicken Thighs:
1. Place chicken thighs in a large bowl and drizzle with coconut oil. Sprinkle with remaining ingredients and toss to coat both sides of thighs.
2. Place thighs skin side up into ungreased zone 2.
Cook:
1. In zone 1, adjust the air fryer temperature to 200ºC and air fry for 22 to 25 minutes.
2. In zone 2, adjust the air fryer temperature to 200ºC and air fry for 25 minutes.
3. Press SYNC, then press Start.
4. For zone 1, flipping chicken halfway through cooking. 4. Transfer chicken to serving platter, tent loosely with aluminum foil, and let rest for 5 minutes. Sprinkle with scallion and serve.
5. For zone 2, after 10 minutes, turn thighs. When 5 minutes remain, flip thighs once more. Chicken will be done when skin is golden brown and the internal temperature is at least 76ºC. Serve warm.

Chicken Schnitzel

Prep time: 15 minutes | Cook time: 5 minutes |
Serves 4

30 g all-purpose flour
1 teaspoon marjoram
½ teaspoon thyme
1 teaspoon dried parsley flakes
½ teaspoon salt
1 egg

1 teaspoon lemon juice
1 teaspoon water
60 g breadcrumbs
4 chicken tenders, pounded
thin, cut in half lengthwise
Cooking spray

1. Preheat the air fryer to 200ºC and spritz with cooking spray. 2. Combine the flour, marjoram, thyme, parsley, and salt in a shallow dish. Stir to mix well. 3. Whisk the egg with lemon juice and water in a large bowl. Pour the breadcrumbs in a separate shallow dish. 4. Roll the chicken halves in the flour mixture first, then in the egg mixture, and then roll over the breadcrumbs to coat well. Shake the excess off. 5. Arrange the chicken halves in the preheated air fryer and spritz with cooking spray on both sides. 6. Air fry for 5 minutes or until the chicken halves are golden brown and crispy. Flip the halves halfway through. 7. Serve immediately.

Ginger Turmeric Chicken Thighs

Prep time: 5 minutes | Cook time: 25 minutes |
Serves 4

4 (115 g) boneless, skin-on
chicken thighs
2 tablespoons coconut oil,
melted
½ teaspoon ground turmeric

½ teaspoon salt
½ teaspoon garlic powder
½ teaspoon ground ginger
¼ teaspoon ground black
pepper

1. Place chicken thighs in a large bowl and drizzle with coconut oil. Sprinkle with remaining ingredients and toss to coat both sides of thighs. 2. Place thighs skin side up into ungreased air fryer basket. Adjust the temperature to 200ºC and air fry for 25 minutes. After 10 minutes, turn thighs. When 5 minutes remain, flip thighs once more. Chicken will be done when skin is golden brown and the internal temperature is at least 76ºC. Serve warm.

Lemon Thyme Roasted Chicken

Prep time: 10 minutes | Cook time: 60 minutes |
Serves 6

2 tablespoons baking powder	80 ml avocado oil
1 teaspoon smoked paprika	120 ml Buffalo hot sauce, such
Sea salt and freshly ground	as Frank's RedHot
black pepper, to taste	4 tablespoons unsalted butter
900 g chicken wings or chicken	2 tablespoons apple cider
drumettes	vinegar
Avocado oil spray	1 teaspoon minced garlic

1. In a large bowl, stir together the baking powder, smoked paprika, and salt and pepper to taste. Add the chicken wings and toss to coat. 2. Set the air fryer to 200°C. Spray the wings with oil. 3. Place them in a single layer half in zone 1, the remaining in zone 2. In zone 1, select Air Fry button, set the time to 20 to 25 minutes. In zone 2, select Match Cook and then press Start. If necessary, working in batches. Check with an instant-read thermometer and remove when they reach 70°C. Let rest until they reach 76°C. 4. While the wings are cooking, whisk together the avocado oil, hot sauce, butter, vinegar, and garlic in a small saucepan over medium-low heat until warm. 5. When the wings are done cooking, toss them with the Buffalo sauce. Serve warm.

Herbed Roast Chicken Breast

Prep time: 10 minutes | Cook time: 25 minutes |
Serves 2 to 4

2 tablespoons salted butter or	½ teaspoon smoked paprika
ghee, at room temperature	¼ teaspoon black pepper
1 teaspoon dried Italian	2 bone-in, skin-on chicken
seasoning, crushed	breast halves (280 g each)
½ teaspoon kosher salt	Lemon wedges, for serving

1. In a small bowl, stir together the butter, Italian seasoning, salt, paprika, and pepper until thoroughly combined. 2. Using a small sharp knife, carefully loosen the skin on each chicken breast half, starting at the thin end of each. Very carefully separate the skin from the flesh, leaving the skin attached at the thick end of each breast. Divide the herb butter into quarters. Rub one-quarter of the butter onto the flesh of each breast. Fold and lightly press the skin back onto each breast. Rub the remaining butter onto the skin of each breast. 3. Place the chicken in one of the air fryer baskets. Set the air fryer to (190°C for 25 minutes. Use a meat thermometer to ensure the chicken breasts have reached an internal temperature of 76°C. 4. Transfer the chicken to a cutting board. Lightly cover with aluminum foil and let rest for 5 to 10 minutes. 5. Serve with lemon wedges.

Broccoli and Cheese Stuffed Chicken & Lemon-Dijon Boneless Chicken

Prep time: 45 minutes | Cook time: 20 minutes

Broccoli and Cheese Stuffed	Lemon-Dijon Boneless Chicken
Chicken | Serves 4:	| Serves 6:
60 g cream cheese, softened	115 g sugar-free mayonnaise
70 g chopped fresh broccoli,	1 tablespoon Dijon mustard
steamed	1 tablespoon freshly squeezed
120 g shredded sharp Cheddar	lemon juice (optional)
cheese	1 tablespoon coconut aminos
4 (170 g) boneless, skinless	1 teaspoon Italian seasoning
chicken breasts	1 teaspoon sea salt
2 tablespoons mayonnaise	½ teaspoon freshly ground
¼ teaspoon salt	black pepper
¼ teaspoon garlic powder	¼ teaspoon cayenne pepper
⅛ teaspoon ground black	680 g boneless, skinless chicken
pepper	breasts or thighs

Prepare for Broccoli and Cheese Stuffed Chicken:
1. In a medium bowl, combine cream cheese, broccoli, and Cheddar. Cut a 4-inch pocket into each chicken breast. Evenly divide mixture between chicken breasts; stuff the pocket of each chicken breast with the mixture.
2. Spread ¼ tablespoon mayonnaise per side of each chicken breast, then sprinkle both sides of breasts with salt, garlic powder, and pepper.
3. Place stuffed chicken breasts into ungreased zone 1 so that the open seams face up.
Prepare for Lemon-Dijon Boneless Chicken:
1. In a small bowl, combine the mayonnaise, mustard, lemon juice (if using), coconut aminos, Italian seasoning, salt, black pepper, and cayenne pepper.
2. Place the chicken in a shallow dish or large zip-top plastic bag. Add the marinade, making sure all the pieces are coated. Cover and refrigerate for at least 30 minutes or up to 4 hours.
3. Arrange the chicken in a single layer in zone 2, working in batches if necessary.
Cook:
1. In zone 1, adjust the air fryer temperature to 180°C and air fry for 20 minutes.
2. In zone 2, adjust the air fryer temperature to 200°C and air fry for 7 minutes.
3. Press SYNC, then press Start.
4. For zone 1, turning chicken halfway through cooking. When done, chicken will be golden and have an internal temperature of at least 76°C. Serve warm.
5. For zone 2, flip the chicken and continue cooking for 6 to 9 minutes more, until an instant-read thermometer reads 70°C.

Indian Fennel Chicken

Prep time: 30 minutes | Cook time: 15 minutes |

Serves 4

450 g boneless, skinless chicken thighs, cut crosswise into thirds
1 yellow onion, cut into 1½-inch-thick slices
1 tablespoon coconut oil, melted
2 teaspoons minced fresh ginger
2 teaspoons minced garlic
1 teaspoon smoked paprika

1 teaspoon ground fennel
1 teaspoon garam masala
1 teaspoon ground turmeric
1 teaspoon kosher salt
½ to 1 teaspoon cayenne pepper
Vegetable oil spray
2 teaspoons fresh lemon juice
5 g chopped fresh coriander or parsley

1. Use a fork to pierce the chicken all over to allow the marinade to penetrate better. 2. In a large bowl, combine the onion, coconut oil, ginger, garlic, paprika, fennel, garam masala, turmeric, salt, and cayenne. Add the chicken, toss to combine, and marinate at room temperature for 30 minutes, or cover and refrigerate for up to 24 hours. 3. Place the chicken and onion in one of the air fryer baskets. (Discard remaining marinade.) Spray with some vegetable oil spray. Set the air fryer to 180°C for 15 minutes. Halfway through the cooking time, remove the basket, spray the chicken and onion with more vegetable oil spray, and toss gently to coat. At the end of the cooking time, use a meat thermometer to ensure the chicken has reached an internal temperature of 76°C. 4. Transfer the chicken and onion to a serving platter. Sprinkle with the lemon juice and coriander and serve.

Fajita-Stuffed Chicken Breast

Prep time: 15 minutes | Cook time: 25 minutes |

Serves 4

2 (170 g) boneless, skinless chicken breasts
¼ medium white onion, peeled and sliced
1 medium green bell pepper,

seeded and sliced
1 tablespoon coconut oil
2 teaspoons chili powder
1 teaspoon ground cumin
½ teaspoon garlic powder

1. Slice each chicken breast completely in half lengthwise into two even pieces. Using a meat tenderizer, pound out the chicken until it's about ¼-inch thickness. 2. Lay each slice of chicken out and place three slices of onion and four slices of green pepper on the end closest to you. Begin rolling the peppers and onions tightly into the chicken. Secure the roll with either toothpicks or a couple pieces of butcher's twine. 3. Drizzle coconut oil over chicken. Sprinkle each side with chili powder, cumin, and garlic powder. Place each roll into one of the air fryer baskets. 4. Adjust the temperature to 180°C and air fry for 25 minutes. 5. Serve warm.

Chicken and Ham Meatballs with Dijon Sauce

Prep time: 10 minutes | Cook time: 15 minutes |

Serves 4

Meatballs:
230 g ham, diced
230 g chicken mince
110 g grated Swiss cheese
1 large egg, beaten
3 cloves garlic, minced
15 g chopped onions
1½ teaspoons sea salt
1 teaspoon ground black pepper
Cooking spray

Dijon Sauce:
3 tablespoons Dijon mustard
2 tablespoons lemon juice
60 ml chicken broth, warmed
¾ teaspoon sea salt
¼ teaspoon ground black pepper
Chopped fresh thyme leaves, for garnish

1. Preheat the air fryer to 200°C. Spritz one of the air fryer baskets with cooking spray. 2. Combine the ingredients for the meatballs in a large bowl. Stir to mix well, then shape the mixture in twelve 1½-inch meatballs. 3. Arrange the meatballs in a single layer in one of the air fryer baskets. Air fry for 15 minutes or until lightly browned. Flip the balls halfway through. You may need to work in batches to avoid overcrowding. 4. Meanwhile, combine the ingredients, except for the thyme leaves, for the sauce in a small bowl. Stir to mix well. 5. Transfer the cooked meatballs on a large plate, then baste the sauce over. Garnish with thyme leaves and serve.

Garlic Soy Chicken Thighs

Prep time: 10 minutes | Cook time: 30 minutes |

Serves 1 to 2

2 tablespoons chicken stock
2 tablespoons reduced-sodium soy sauce
1½ tablespoons sugar
4 garlic cloves, smashed and peeled

2 large spring onions, cut into 2- to 3-inch batons, plus more, thinly sliced, for garnish
2 bone-in, skin-on chicken thighs (198 to 225 g each)

1. Preheat the air fryer to 190°C. 2. In a metal cake pan, combine the chicken stock, soy sauce, and sugar and stir until the sugar dissolves. Add the garlic cloves, spring onions, and chicken thighs, turning the thighs to coat them in the marinade, then resting them skin-side up. Place the pan in the air fryer and bake, flipping the thighs every 5 minutes after the first 10 minutes, until the chicken is cooked through and the marinade is reduced to a sticky glaze over the chicken, about 30 minutes. 3. Remove the pan from the air fryer and serve the chicken thighs warm, with any remaining glaze spooned over top and sprinkled with more sliced spring onions.

Chicken Pesto Parmigiana

Prep time: 10 minutes | Cook time: 23 minutes | Serves 4

2 large eggs	pounded to ¼ inch thick
1 tablespoon water	65 g pesto
Fine sea salt and ground black pepper, to taste	115 g shredded Mozzarella cheese
45 g powdered Parmesan cheese	Finely chopped fresh basil, for garnish (optional)
2 teaspoons Italian seasoning	Grape tomatoes, halved, for serving (optional)
4 (140 g) boneless, skinless chicken breasts or thighs,	

1. Spray one of the air fryer baskets with avocado oil. Preheat the air fryer to 200°C. 2. Crack the eggs into a shallow baking dish, add the water and a pinch each of salt and pepper, and whisk to combine. In another shallow baking dish, stir together the Parmesan and Italian seasoning until well combined. 3. Season the chicken breasts well on both sides with salt and pepper. Dip one chicken breast in the eggs and let any excess drip off, then dredge both sides of the breast in the Parmesan mixture. Spray the breast with avocado oil and place it in one of the air fryer baskets. Repeat with the remaining 3 chicken breasts. 4. Air fry the chicken in the air fryer for 20 minutes, or until the internal temperature reaches 76°C and the breading is golden brown, flipping halfway through. 5. Dollop each chicken breast with ¼ of the pesto and top with the Mozzarella. Return the breasts to the air fryer and cook for 3 minutes, or until the cheese is melted. Garnish with basil and serve with halved grape tomatoes on the side, if desired. 6. Store leftovers in an airtight container in the refrigerator for up to 4 days. Reheat in a preheated 200°C air fryer for 5 minutes, or until warmed through.

Buttermilk-Fried Drumsticks

Prep time: 10 minutes | Cook time: 25 minutes | Serves 2

1 egg	1 teaspoon salt
120 g buttermilk	¼ teaspoon ground black pepper (to mix into coating)
45 g self-rising flour	
45 g seasoned panko bread crumbs	4 chicken drumsticks, skin on
	Oil for misting or cooking spray

1. Beat together egg and buttermilk in shallow dish. 2. In a second shallow dish, combine the flour, panko crumbs, salt, and pepper. 3. Sprinkle chicken legs with additional salt and pepper to taste. 4. Dip legs in buttermilk mixture, then roll in panko mixture, pressing in crumbs to make coating stick. Mist with oil or cooking spray. 5. Spray one of the air fryer baskets with cooking spray. 6. Cook drumsticks at 180°C for 10 minutes. Turn pieces over and cook an additional 10 minutes. 7. Turn pieces to check for browning. If you have any white spots that haven't begun to brown, spritz them with oil or cooking spray. Continue cooking for 5 more minutes or until crust is golden brown and juices run clear. Larger, meatier drumsticks will take longer to cook than small ones.

Classic Whole Chicken & Spice-Rubbed Chicken Thighs

Prep time: 15 minutes | Cook time: 50 minutes

Classic Whole Chicken | Serves 4:	fresh parsley, for garnish
Oil, for spraying	Spice-Rubbed Chicken Thighs | Serves 4:
1 (1.8 kg) whole chicken, giblets removed	4 (115 g) bone-in, skin-on chicken thighs
1 tablespoon olive oil	½ teaspoon salt
1 teaspoon paprika	½ teaspoon garlic powder
½ teaspoon granulated garlic	2 teaspoons chili powder
½ teaspoon salt	1 teaspoon paprika
½ teaspoon freshly ground black pepper	1 teaspoon ground cumin
¼ teaspoon finely chopped	1 small lime, halved

Prepare for Classic Whole Chicken:
1. Line zone 1 drawer with parchment and spray lightly with oil.
2. Pat the chicken dry with paper towels. Rub it with the olive oil until evenly coated.
3. In a small bowl, mix together the paprika, garlic, salt, and black pepper and sprinkle it evenly over the chicken.
4. Place the chicken in the prepared basket, breast-side down.
Prepare for Spice-Rubbed Chicken Thighs:
1. Pat chicken thighs dry and sprinkle with salt, garlic powder, chili powder, paprika, and cumin.
2. Squeeze juice from ½ lime over thighs. Place thighs into ungreased zone 2.
Cook:
1. In zone 1, adjust the air fryer temperature to 180°C and air fry for 30 minutes.
2. In zone 2, adjust the air fryer temperature to 190°C and air fry for 25 minutes.
3. Press SYNC, then press Start.
4. For zone 1, flip, and cook for another 20 minutes, or until the internal temperature reaches 76°C and the juices run clear. Sprinkle with the parsley before serving.
5. For zone 2, turning thighs halfway through cooking. Thighs will be crispy and browned with an internal temperature of at least 76°C when done. Transfer thighs to a large serving plate and drizzle with remaining lime juice. Serve warm.

Italian Chicken with Sauce

Prep time: 15 minutes | Cook time: 20 minutes | Serves 4

2 large skinless chicken breasts (about 565 g)
Salt and freshly ground black pepper
25 g almond meal
45 g grated Parmesan cheese
2 teaspoons Italian seasoning

1 egg, lightly beaten
1 tablespoon olive oil
225 g no-sugar-added marinara sauce
4 slices Mozzarella cheese or 110 g shredded Mozzarella

1. Preheat the air fryer to 180°C. 2. Slice the chicken breasts in half horizontally to create 4 thinner chicken breasts. Working with one piece at a time, place the chicken between two pieces of parchment paper and pound with a meat mallet or rolling pin to flatten to an even thickness. Season both sides with salt and freshly ground black pepper. 3. In a large shallow bowl, combine the almond meal, Parmesan, and Italian seasoning; stir until thoroughly combined. Place the egg in another large shallow bowl. 4. Dip the chicken in the egg, followed by the almond meal mixture, pressing the mixture firmly into the chicken to create an even coating. 5. Working in batches if necessary, arrange the chicken breasts in a single layer in one of the air fryer baskets and coat both sides lightly with olive oil. Pausing halfway through the cooking time to flip the chicken, air fry for 15 minutes, or until a thermometer inserted into the thickest part registers 76°C. 6. Spoon the marinara sauce over each piece of chicken and top with the Mozzarella cheese. Air fry for an additional 3 to 5 minutes until the cheese is melted.

Italian Flavour Chicken Breasts with Roma Tomatoes

Prep time: 10 minutes | Cook time: 60 minutes | Serves 8

1.4 kg chicken breasts, bone-in
1 teaspoon minced fresh basil
1 teaspoon minced fresh rosemary
2 tablespoons minced fresh parsley
1 teaspoon cayenne pepper

½ teaspoon salt
½ teaspoon freshly ground black pepper
4 medium Roma tomatoes, halved
Cooking spray

1. Preheat the air fryer to 190°C. Spritz the air fryer basket with cooking spray. 2. Combine all the ingredients, except for the chicken breasts and tomatoes, in a large bowl. Stir to mix well. 3. Dunk the chicken breasts in the mixture and press to coat well. 4. Place them half in zone 1, the remaining in zone 2. In zone 1, select Air Fry button, set the time to 25 minutes. In zone 2, select

Match Cook and then press Start. You may need to work in batches to avoid overcrowding. 5. Flip the breasts halfway through the cooking time. 6. Remove the cooked chicken breasts from the basket and adjust the temperature to 180°C. 7. Place the tomatoes in the air fryer and spritz with cooking spray. Sprinkle with a touch of salt and cook for 10 minutes or until tender. Shake the basket halfway through the cooking time. 8. Serve the tomatoes with chicken breasts on a large serving plate.

Chicken Shawarma & Chicken Nuggets

Prep time: 40 minutes | Cook time: 15 minutes

Chicken Shawarma | Serves 4:
Shawarma Spice:
2 teaspoons dried oregano
1 teaspoon ground cinnamon
1 teaspoon ground cumin
1 teaspoon ground coriander
1 teaspoon kosher salt
½ teaspoon ground allspice
½ teaspoon cayenne pepper
Chicken:
450 g boneless, skinless chicken thighs, cut into large bite-size chunks

2 tablespoons vegetable oil
For Serving:
Tzatziki
Pita bread
Chicken Nuggets | Serves 4:
450 g chicken mince thighs
110 g shredded Mozzarella cheese
1 large egg, whisked
½ teaspoon salt
¼ teaspoon dried oregano
¼ teaspoon garlic powder

Prepare for Chicken Shawarma:
1. For the shawarma spice: In a small bowl, combine the oregano, cayenne, cumin, coriander, salt, cinnamon, and allspice.
2. For the chicken: In a large bowl, toss together the chicken, vegetable oil, and shawarma spice to coat. Marinate at room temperature for 30 minutes or cover and refrigerate for up to 24 hours.
3. Place the chicken in zone 1.
Prepare for Chicken Nuggets:
1. In a large bowl, combine all ingredients. Form mixture into twenty nugget shapes, about 2 tablespoons each.
2. Place nuggets into ungreased zone 2, working in batches if needed.
Cook:
1. In zone 1, adjust the air fryer temperature to 180°C and air fry for 15 minutes, or until the chicken reaches an internal temperature of 76°C
2. In zone 2, adjust the air fryer temperature to 190°C and air fry for 15 minutes.
3. Press SYNC, then press Start.
4. For zone 1, transfer the chicken to a serving platter. Serve with tzatziki and pita bread.
5. For zone 2, turning nuggets halfway through cooking. Let cool 5 minutes before serving.

Yakitori

Prep time: 10 minutes | Cook time: 15 minutes |
Serves 4

120 ml mirin
60 ml dry white wine
120 ml soy sauce
1 tablespoon light brown sugar
680 g boneless, skinless chicken thighs, cut into 1½-inch pieces, fat trimmed
4 medium spring onions,

trimmed, cut into 1½-inch pieces
Cooking spray
Special Equipment:
4 (4-inch) bamboo skewers, soaked in water for at least 30 minutes

1. Combine the mirin, dry white wine, soy sauce, and brown sugar in a saucepan. Bring to a boil over medium heat. Keep stirring. 2. Boil for another 2 minutes or until it has a thick consistency. Turn off the heat. 3. Preheat the air fryer to 200ºC. Spritz one of the air fryer baskets with cooking spray. 4. Run the bamboo skewers through the chicken pieces and spring onions alternatively. 5. Arrange the skewers in the preheated air fryer, then brush with mirin mixture on both sides. Spritz with cooking spray. 6. Air fry for 10 minutes or until the chicken and spring onions are glossy. Flip the skewers halfway through. 7. Serve immediately.

Spinach and Feta Stuffed Chicken Breasts

Prep time: 10 minutes | Cook time: 27 minutes |
Serves 4

1 (280 g) package frozen spinach, thawed and drained well
80 g feta cheese, crumbled
½ teaspoon freshly ground

black pepper
4 boneless chicken breasts
Salt and freshly ground black pepper, to taste
1 tablespoon olive oil

1. Prepare the filling. Squeeze out as much liquid as possible from the thawed spinach. Rough chop the spinach and transfer it to a mixing bowl with the feta cheese and the freshly ground black pepper. 2. Prepare the chicken breast. Place the chicken breast on a cutting board and press down on the chicken breast with one hand to keep it stabilized. Make an incision about 1-inch long in the fattest side of the breast. Move the knife up and down inside the chicken breast, without poking through either the top or the bottom, or the other side of the breast. The inside pocket should be about 3-inches long, but the opening should only be about 1-inch wide. If this is too difficult, you can make the incision longer, but you will have to be more careful when cooking the chicken breast since this will expose more of the stuffing. 3. Once you have prepared the chicken breasts, use your fingers to stuff the filling into each pocket,

spreading the mixture down as far as you can. 4. Preheat the air fryer to 190ºC. 5. Lightly brush or spray one of the air fryer baskets and the chicken breasts with olive oil. Transfer two of the stuffed chicken breasts to the air fryer. Air fry for 12 minutes, turning the chicken breasts over halfway through the cooking time. Remove the chicken to a resting plate and air fry the second two breasts for 12 minutes. Return the first batch of chicken to the air fryer with the second batch and air fry for 3 more minutes. When the chicken is cooked, an instant read thermometer should register 76ºC in the thickest part of the chicken, as well as in the stuffing. 6. Remove the chicken breasts and let them rest on a cutting board for 2 to 3 minutes. Slice the chicken on the bias and serve with the slices fanned out.

Spicy Chicken Thighs and Gold Potatoes

Prep time: 5 minutes | Cook time: 25 minutes |
Serves 4

4 bone-in, skin-on chicken thighs
½ teaspoon kosher salt or ¼ teaspoon fine salt
2 tablespoons melted unsalted butter
2 teaspoons Worcestershire sauce
2 teaspoons curry powder
1 teaspoon dried oregano leaves

½ teaspoon dry mustard
½ teaspoon granulated garlic
¼ teaspoon paprika
¼ teaspoon hot pepper sauce
Cooking oil spray
4 medium Yukon gold potatoes, chopped
1 tablespoon extra-virgin olive oil

1. Sprinkle the chicken thighs on both sides with salt. 2. In a medium bowl, stir together the melted butter, Worcestershire sauce, curry powder, oregano, dry mustard, granulated garlic, paprika, and hot pepper sauce. Add the thighs to the sauce and stir to coat. 3. Insert the crisper plate into the basket and the basket into the unit. Preheat the unit by selecting AIR FRY, setting the temperature to 200ºC, and setting the time to 3 minutes. Select START/STOP to begin. 4. Once the unit is preheated, spray the crisper plate with cooking oil. In the basket, combine the potatoes and olive oil and toss to coat. 5. Add the wire rack to the air fryer and place the chicken thighs on top. 6. Select AIR FRY, set the temperature to 200ºC, and set the time to 25 minutes. Select START/STOP to begin. 7. After 19 minutes check the chicken thighs. If a food thermometer inserted into the chicken registers 76ºC, transfer them to a clean plate, and cover with aluminum foil to keep warm. If they aren't cooked to 76ºC, resume cooking for another 1 to 2 minutes until they are done. Remove them from the unit along with the rack. 8. Remove the basket and shake it to distribute the potatoes. Reinsert the basket to resume cooking for 3 to 6 minutes, or until the potatoes are crisp and golden brown. 9. When the cooking is complete, serve the chicken with the potatoes.

Gold Livers

Prep time: 10 minutes | Cook time: 20 minutes | Serves 4

2 eggs
2 tablespoons water
45 g flour
120 g panko breadcrumbs
1 teaspoon salt

½ teaspoon ground black pepper
570 g chicken livers
Cooking spray

1. Preheat the air fryer to 200°C. Spritz one of the air fryer baskets with cooking spray. 2. Whisk the eggs with water in a large bowl. Pour the flour in a separate bowl. Pour the panko on a shallow dish and sprinkle with salt and pepper. 3. Dredge the chicken livers in the flour. Shake the excess off, then dunk the livers in the whisked eggs, and then roll the livers over the panko to coat well. 4. Arrange the livers in the preheated air fryer and spritz with cooking spray. Work in batches to avoid overcrowding. 5. Air fry for 10 minutes or until the livers are golden and crispy. Flip the livers halfway through. Repeat with remaining livers. 6. Serve immediately.

Chicken Hand Pies

Prep time: 30 minutes | Cook time: 10 minutes per batch | Makes 8 pies

180 ml chicken broth
130 g frozen mixed peas and carrots
140 g cooked chicken, chopped
1 tablespoon cornflour

1 tablespoon milk
Salt and pepper, to taste
1 (8-count) can organic flaky biscuits
Oil for misting or cooking spray

1. In a medium saucepan, bring chicken broth to a boil. Stir in the frozen peas and carrots and cook for 5 minutes over medium heat. Stir in chicken. 2. Mix the cornflour into the milk until it dissolves. Stir it into the simmering chicken broth mixture and cook just until thickened. 3. Remove from heat, add salt and pepper to taste, and let cool slightly. 4. Lay biscuits out on wax paper. Peel each biscuit apart in the middle to make 2 rounds so you have 16 rounds total.

Using your hands or a rolling pin, flatten each biscuit round slightly to make it larger and thinner. 5. Divide chicken filling among 8 of the biscuit rounds. Place remaining biscuit rounds on top and press edges all around. Use the tines of a fork to crimp biscuit edges and make sure they are sealed well. 6. Spray both sides lightly with oil or cooking spray. 7. Cook in a single layer, 4 at a time, at 170°C for 10 minutes or until biscuit dough is cooked through and golden brown.

Sesame Chicken Breast

Prep time: 10 minutes | Cook time: 18 minutes | Serves 6

Oil, for spraying
2 (170 g) boneless, skinless chicken breasts, cut into bite-size pieces
30 g cornflour plus 1 tablespoon
60 ml soy sauce
2 tablespoons packed light

brown sugar
2 tablespoons pineapple juice
1 tablespoon molasses
½ teaspoon ground ginger
1 tablespoon water
2 teaspoons sesame seeds

1. Line the air fryer basket with parchment and spray lightly with oil. 2. Place the chicken and 60 g of cornflour in a zip-top plastic bag, seal, and shake well until evenly coated. 3. Place them in an even layer half in zone 1, the remaining in zone 2. Spray liberally with oil. In zone 1, select Air Fry button, air fry at 200°C for 9 minutes. In zone 2, select Match Cook and then press Start. You may need to work in batches, depending on the size of your fryer. 4. flip, spray with more oil, and cook for another 8 to 9 minutes, or until the internal temperature reaches 76°C. 5. In a small saucepan, combine the soy sauce, brown sugar, pineapple juice, molasses, and ginger over medium heat and cook, stirring frequently, until the brown sugar has dissolved. 6. In a small bowl, mix together the water and remaining 1 tablespoon of cornflour. Pour it into the soy sauce mixture. 7. Bring the mixture to a boil, stirring frequently, until the sauce thickens. Remove from the heat. 8. Transfer the chicken to a large bowl, add the sauce, and toss until evenly coated. Sprinkle with the sesame seeds and serve.

Chapter 5 Fish and Seafood

Chapter 5 Fish and Seafood

Thai Prawn Skewers with Peanut Dipping Sauce

Prep time: 15 minutes | Cook time: 6 minutes |
Serves 2

Salt and pepper, to taste	6 (6-inch) wooden skewers
340 g extra-large prawns, peeled and deveined	3 tablespoons creamy peanut butter
1 tablespoon vegetable oil	3 tablespoons hot tap water
1 teaspoon honey	1 tablespoon chopped fresh coriander
½ teaspoon grated lime zest plus 1 tablespoon juice, plus lime wedges for serving	1 teaspoon fish sauce

1. Preheat the air fryer to 200ºC. 2. Dissolve 2 tablespoons salt in 1 litre cold water in a large container. Add prawns, cover, and refrigerate for 15 minutes. 3. Remove prawns from brine and pat dry with paper towels. Whisk oil, honey, lime zest, and ¼ teaspoon pepper together in a large bowl. Add prawns and toss to coat. Thread prawns onto skewers, leaving about ¼ inch between each prawns (3 or 4 prawns per skewer). 4. Arrange 3 skewers in air fryer basket, parallel to each other and spaced evenly apart. Arrange remaining 3 skewers on top, perpendicular to the bottom layer. Air fry until prawns are opaque throughout, 6 to 8 minutes, flipping and rotating skewers halfway through cooking. 5. Whisk peanut butter, hot tap water, lime juice, coriander, and fish sauce together in a bowl until smooth. Serve skewers with peanut dipping sauce and lime wedges.

Sea Bass with Potato Scales

Prep time: 10 minutes | Cook time: 10 minutes |
Serves 2

2 fillets of sea bass, 170- to 230 g each	2 Fingerling, or new potatoes, very thinly sliced into rounds
Salt and freshly ground black pepper, to taste	Olive oil
60 ml mayonnaise	½ clove garlic, crushed into a paste
2 teaspoons finely chopped lemon zest	1 tablespoon capers, drained and rinsed
1 teaspoon chopped fresh thyme	1 tablespoon olive oil

1 teaspoon lemon juice, to taste

1. Preheat the air fryer to 200ºC. 2. Season the fish well with salt and freshly ground black pepper. Mix the mayonnaise, lemon zest and thyme together in a small bowl. Spread a thin layer of the mayonnaise mixture on both fillets. Start layering rows of potato slices onto the fish fillets to simulate the fish scales. The second row should overlap the first row slightly. Dabbing a little more mayonnaise along the upper edge of the row of potatoes where the next row overlaps will help the potato slices stick. Press the potatoes onto the fish to secure them well and season again with salt. Brush or spray the potato layer with olive oil. 3. Transfer the fish to the air fryer and air fry for 8 to 10 minutes, depending on the thickness of your fillets. 1-inch of fish should take 10 minutes at 200ºC. 4. While the fish is cooking, add the garlic, capers, olive oil and lemon juice to the remaining mayonnaise mixture to make the caper aïoli. 5. Serve the fish warm with a dollop of the aïoli on top or on the side.

Panko Crab Sticks with Mayo Sauce

Prep time: 5 minutes | Cook time: 12 minutes |
Serves 4

Crab Sticks:	Cooking spray
2 eggs	Mayo Sauce:
120 g plain flour	115 g mayonnaise
50 g panko bread crumbs	1 lime, juiced
1 tablespoon Old Bay seasoning	2 garlic cloves, minced
455 g crab sticks	

1. Preheat air fryer to 200ºC. 2. In a bowl, beat the eggs. In a shallow bowl, place the flour. In another shallow bowl, thoroughly combine the panko bread crumbs and old bay seasoning. 3. Dredge the crab sticks in the flour, shaking off any excess, then in the beaten eggs, finally press them in the bread crumb mixture to coat well. 4. Arrange the crab sticks in one of the air fryer baskets and spray with cooking spray. 5. Air fry for 12 minutes until golden brown. Flip the crab sticks halfway through the cooking time. 6. Meanwhile, make the sauce by whisking together the mayo, lime juice, and garlic in a small bowl. 7. Serve the crab sticks with the mayo sauce on the side.

Balsamic Tilapia & Fried Prawns

Prep time: 20 minutes | Cook time: 20 minutes

Balsamic Tilapia | Serves 4:
4 tilapia fillets, boneless
2 tablespoons balsamic vinegar
1 teaspoon avocado oil
1 teaspoon dried basil
Fried Prawns | Serves 4:
35 g self-raising flour
1 teaspoon paprika
1 teaspoon salt

½ teaspoon freshly ground
black pepper
1 large egg, beaten
60 g finely crushed panko bread
crumbs
20 frozen large prawns (about
900 g), peeled and deveined
Cooking spray

Prepare for Balsamic Tilapia:
1. Sprinkle the tilapia fillets with balsamic vinegar, avocado oil, and dried basil. 2. Then put the fillets in zone 1.
Prepare for Fried Prawns:
1. In a shallow bowl, whisk the flour, paprika, salt, and pepper until blended. Add the beaten egg to a second shallow bowl and the bread crumbs to a third.
2. One at a time, dip the prawns into the flour, the egg, and the bread crumbs, coating thoroughly.
3. Line zone 2 with baking paper.
4. Place the prawns on the baking paper and spritz with oil.
Cook:
1. In zone 1, adjust the air fryer temperature to 200°C and air fry for 15 minutes.
2. In zone 2, adjust the air fryer temperature to 200°C and air fry for 2 minutes.
3. Press SYNC, then press Start.
4. For zone 2, shake the basket, spritz the prawns with oil, and air fry for 3 minutes more until lightly browned and crispy. Serve hot.

Snapper Scampi & Tandoori Prawns

Prep time: 30 minutes | Cook time: 10 minutes

Snapper Scampi | Serves 4:
4 skinless snapper or arctic char fillets, 170 g each
1 tablespoon olive oil
3 tablespoons lemon juice, divided
½ teaspoon dried basil
Pinch salt
Freshly ground black pepper, to taste
2 tablespoons butter
2 cloves garlic, minced
Tandoori Prawns | Serves 4:

455 g jumbo raw prawns (21 to 25 count), peeled and deveined
1 tablespoon minced fresh ginger
3 cloves garlic, minced
5 g chopped fresh coriander or parsley, plus more for garnish
1 teaspoon ground turmeric
1 teaspoon garam masala
1 teaspoon smoked paprika
1 teaspoon kosher or coarse sea salt
½ to 1 teaspoon cayenne pepper

2 tablespoons olive oil (for Paleo) or melted ghee

2 teaspoons fresh lemon juice

Prepare for Snapper Scampi:
1. Rub the fish fillets with olive oil and 1 tablespoon of the lemon juice. Sprinkle with the basil, salt, and pepper, and place in zone 1.
Prepare for Tandoori Prawns:
1. In a large bowl, combine the prawns, ginger, garlic, coriander, turmeric, garam masala, paprika, salt, and cayenne. Toss well to coat. Add the oil or ghee and toss again. Marinate at room temperature for 15 minutes, or cover and refrigerate for up to 8 hours.
2. Place the prawns in a single layer in zone 2.
Cook:
1. In zone 1, adjust the air fryer temperature to 190°C and air fry for 7 to 8 minutes, or until the fish just flakes when tested with a fork.
2. In zone 2, adjust the air fryer temperature to 160°C and air fry for 6 minutes.
3. Press SYNC, then press Start.
4. For zone 1, remove the fish from the basket and put on a serving plate. Cover to keep warm. In a baking pan, combine the butter, remaining 2 tablespoons lemon juice, and garlic. Bake in the air fryer for 1 to 2 minutes or until the garlic is sizzling. Pour this mixture over the fish and serve.
5. For zone 2, transfer the prawns to a serving platter. Cover and let the prawns finish cooking in the residual heat, about 5 minutes. Sprinkle the prawns with the lemon juice and toss to coat. Garnish with additional cilantro and serve.

Pecan-Crusted Catfish

Prep time: 5 minutes | Cook time: 12 minutes | Serves 4

65 g pecans, finely crushed
1 teaspoon fine sea salt
¼ teaspoon ground black pepper

4 catfish fillets, 110g each
For Garnish (Optional):
Fresh oregano
Pecan halves

1. Spray one of the air fryer baskets with avocado oil. Preheat the air fryer to 190°C. 2. In a large bowl, mix the crushed pecan, salt, and pepper. One at a time, dredge the catfish fillets in the mixture, coating them well. Use your hands to press the pecan meal into the fillets. Spray the fish with avocado oil and place them in one of the air fryer baskets. 3. Air fry the coated catfish for 12 minutes, or until it flakes easily and is no longer translucent in the center, flipping halfway through. 4. Garnish with oregano sprigs and pecan halves, if desired. 5. Store leftovers in an airtight container in the fridge for up to 3 days. Reheat in a preheated 180°C air fryer for 4 minutes, or until heated through.

Prawn and Cherry Tomato Kebabs

Prep time: 15 minutes | Cook time: 5 minutes | Serves 4

680 g jumbo prawns, cleaned, peeled and deveined
455 g cherry tomatoes
2 tablespoons butter, melted
1 tablespoons Sriracha sauce
Sea salt and ground black pepper, to taste
1 teaspoon dried parsley flakes
½ teaspoon dried basil
½ teaspoon dried oregano
½ teaspoon mustard seeds
½ teaspoon marjoram
Special Equipment:
4 to 6 wooden skewers, soaked in water for 30 minutes

1. Preheat the air fryer to 200ºC. 2. Put all the ingredients in a large bowl and toss to coat well. 3. Make the kebabs: Thread, alternating jumbo prawns and cherry tomatoes, onto the wooden skewers that fit into the air fryer. 4. Arrange the kebabs in one of the air fryer baskets. You may need to cook in batches depending on the size of your air fryer basket. 5. Air fry for 5 minutes, or until the prawns are pink and the cherry tomatoes are softened. Repeat with the remaining kebabs. Let the prawns and cherry tomato kebabs cool for 5 minutes and serve hot.

Lemon Pepper Prawns & Oregano Tilapia Fingers

Prep time: 30 minutes | Cook time: 9 minutes

Lemon Pepper Prawns | Serves 2:
Olive or vegetable oil, for spraying
340 g medium raw prawns, peeled and deveined
3 tablespoons lemon juice
1 tablespoon olive oil
1 teaspoon lemon pepper
¼ teaspoon paprika
¼ teaspoon granulated garlic
Oregano Tilapia Fingers | Serves 4:
455 g tilapia fillet
30 g coconut flour
2 eggs, beaten
½ teaspoon ground paprika
1 teaspoon dried oregano
1 teaspoon avocado oil

Prepare for Lemon Pepper Prawns:
1. Preheat the air fryer to 200ºC. Line zone 1 drawer with baking paper and spray lightly with oil.
2. In a medium bowl, toss together the prawns, lemon juice, olive oil, lemon pepper, paprika, and garlic until evenly coated.
3. Place the prawns in the prepared basket.
Prepare for Oregano Tilapia Fingers:
1. Cut the tilapia fillets into fingers and sprinkle with ground paprika and dried oregano.
2. Then dip the tilapia fingers in eggs and coat in the coconut flour.
3. Sprinkle fish fingers with avocado oil and cook in zone 2.

Cook:
1. In zone 1, adjust the air fryer temperature to 200ºC and air fry for 6 to 8 minutes, or until pink and firm.
2. In zone 2, adjust the air fryer temperature to 190ºC and air fry for 9 minutes.
3. Press SYNC, then press Start.

Tuna and Fruit Kebabs & Garlicky Cod Fillets

Prep time: 25 minutes | Cook time: 12 minutes

Tuna and Fruit Kebabs | Serves 4:
455 g tuna steaks, cut into 1-inch cubes
85 g canned pineapple chunks, drained, juice reserved
75 g large red grapes
1 tablespoon honey
2 teaspoons grated fresh ginger
1 teaspoon olive oil
Pinch cayenne pepper
Garlicky Cod Fillets | Serves 4:
1 teaspoon olive oil
4 cod fillets
¼ teaspoon fine sea salt
¼ teaspoon ground black pepper, or more to taste
1 teaspoon cayenne pepper
8 g fresh Italian parsley, coarsely chopped
120 ml milk
1 Italian pepper, chopped
4 garlic cloves, minced
1 teaspoon dried basil
½ teaspoon dried oregano

Prepare for Tuna and Fruit Kebabs:
1. Thread the tuna, pineapple, and grapes on 8 bamboo or 4 metal skewers that fit in zone 1 drawer.
2. In a small bowl, whisk the honey, 1 tablespoon of reserved pineapple juice, the ginger, olive oil, and cayenne. Brush this mixture over the kebabs. Let them stand for 10 minutes.
Prepare for Garlicky Cod Fillets:
1. Lightly coat the sides and bottom of a baking dish with the olive oil. Set aside.
2. In a large bowl, sprinkle the fillets with salt, black pepper, and cayenne pepper.
3. In a food processor, pulse the remaining ingredients until smoothly puréed.
4. Add the purée to the bowl of fillets and toss to coat, then transfer to the prepared baking dish.
5. Preheat the air fryer to 190ºC.
6. Put the baking dish in zone 2.
Cook:
1. In zone 1, adjust the air fryer temperature to 190ºC and air fry for 8 to 12 minutes, or until the tuna reaches an internal temperature of at least 64ºC on a meat thermometer, and the fruit is tender and glazed, brushing once with the remaining sauce.
2. In zone 2, adjust the air fryer temperature to 170ºC and air fry for 10 to 12 minutes, or until the fish flakes when pressed lightly with a fork.
3. Press SYNC, then press Start.

Cod with Jalapeño & Mackerel with Spinach

Prep time: 20 minutes | Cook time: 20 minutes

Cod with Jalapeño | Serves 4:
4 cod fillets, boneless
1 jalapeño, minced
1 tablespoon avocado oil
½ teaspoon minced garlic
Mackerel with Spinach | Serves 5:

455 g mackerel, trimmed
1 bell pepper, chopped
15 g spinach, chopped
1 tablespoon avocado oil
1 teaspoon ground black pepper
1 teaspoon tomato paste

Prepare for Cod with Jalapeño:
1. In the shallow bowl, mix minced jalapeño, avocado oil, and minced garlic.
2. Put the cod fillets in zone 1 in one layer and top with minced jalapeño mixture.
Prepare for Mackerel with Spinach:
1. In the mixing bowl, mix bell pepper with spinach, ground black pepper, and tomato paste.
2. Fill the mackerel with spinach mixture.
3. Then brush the fish with avocado oil and put it in zone 2.
Cook:
1. In zone 1, adjust the air fryer temperature to 190ºC and air fry for 7 minutes per side.
2. In zone 2, adjust the air fryer temperature to 190ºC and air fry for 20 minutes.
3. Press SYNC, then press Start.

Marinated Swordfish Skewers

Prep time: 30 minutes | Cook time: 6 to 8 minutes | Serves 4

455 g filleted swordfish
60 ml avocado oil
2 tablespoons freshly squeezed lemon juice
1 tablespoon minced fresh

parsley
2 teaspoons Dijon mustard
Sea salt and freshly ground black pepper, to taste
85 g cherry tomatoes

1. Cut the fish into 1½-inch chunks, picking out any remaining bones. 2. In a large bowl, whisk together the oil, lemon juice, parsley, and Dijon mustard. Season to taste with salt and pepper. Add the fish and toss to coat the pieces. Cover and marinate the fish chunks in the refrigerator for 30 minutes. 3. Remove the fish from the marinade. Thread the fish and cherry tomatoes on 4 skewers, alternating as you go. 4. Set the air fryer to 200ºC. Place the skewers in one of the air fryer baskets and air fry for 3 minutes. Flip the skewers and cook for 3 to 5 minutes longer, until the fish is cooked through and an instant-read thermometer reads 60ºC.

Tuna Patties with Spicy Sriracha Sauce

Prep time: 10 minutes | Cook time: 10 minutes | Serves 4

2 (170 g) cans tuna packed in oil, drained
3 tablespoons almond flour
2 tablespoons mayonnaise
1 teaspoon dried dill
½ teaspoon onion powder

Pinch of salt and pepper
Spicy Sriracha Sauce:
60 g mayonnaise
1 tablespoon Sriracha sauce
1 teaspoon garlic powder

1. Preheat the air fryer to 190ºC. Line the basket with baking paper. 2. In a large bowl, combine the tuna, almond flour, mayonnaise, dill, and onion powder. Season to taste with salt and freshly ground black pepper. Use a fork to stir, mashing with the back of the fork as necessary, until thoroughly combined. 3. Use an ice cream scoop to form the tuna mixture patties. Place the patties in a single layer on the baking paper in one of the air fryer baskets. Press lightly with the bottom of the scoop to flatten into a circle about ½ inch thick. Pausing halfway through the cooking time to turn the patties, air fry for 10 minutes until lightly browned. 4. To make the Sriracha sauce: In a small bowl, combine the mayonnaise, Sriracha, and garlic powder. Serve the tuna patties topped with the Sriracha sauce.

Fried Catfish with Dijon Sauce

Prep time: 20 minutes | Cook time: 7 minutes | Serves 4

4 tablespoons butter, melted
2 teaspoons Worcestershire sauce, divided
1 teaspoon lemon pepper
60 g panko bread crumbs

4 catfish fillets, 110g each
Cooking spray
120 ml sour cream
1 tablespoon Dijon mustard

1. In a shallow bowl, stir together the melted butter, 1 teaspoon of Worcestershire sauce, and the lemon pepper. Place the bread crumbs in another shallow bowl. 2. One at a time, dip both sides of the fillets in the butter mixture, then the bread crumbs, coating thoroughly. 3. Preheat the air fryer to 150ºC. Line one of the air fryer baskets with baking paper. 4. Place the coated fish on the baking paper and spritz with oil. 5. Bake for 4 minutes. Flip the fish, spritz it with oil, and bake for 3 to 6 minutes more, depending on the thickness of the fillets, until the fish flakes easily with a fork. 6. In a small bowl, stir together the sour cream, Dijon, and remaining 1 teaspoon of Worcestershire sauce. This sauce can be made 1 day in advance and refrigerated before serving. Serve with the fried fish.

Crunchy Air Fried Cod Fillets

Prep time: 10 minutes | Cook time: 12 minutes | Serves 2

20 g panko bread crumbs
1 teaspoon vegetable oil
1 small shallot, minced
1 small garlic clove, minced
½ teaspoon minced fresh thyme
Salt and pepper, to taste
1 tablespoon minced fresh parsley
1 tablespoon mayonnaise
1 large egg yolk
¼ teaspoon grated lemon zest, plus lemon wedges for serving
2 (230 g) skinless cod fillets, 1¼ inches thick
Vegetable oil spray

1. Preheat the air fryer to 150ºC. 2. Make foil sling for air fryer basket by folding 1 long sheet of aluminum foil so it is 4 inches wide. Lay sheet of foil widthwise across basket, pressing foil into and up sides of basket. Fold excess foil as needed so that edges of foil are flush with top of basket. Lightly spray the foil and basket with vegetable oil spray. 3. Toss the panko with the oil in a bowl until evenly coated. Stir in the shallot, garlic, thyme, ¼ teaspoon salt, and ⅛ teaspoon pepper. Microwave, stirring frequently, until the panko is light golden brown, about 2 minutes. Transfer to a shallow dish and let cool slightly; stir in the parsley. Whisk the mayonnaise, egg yolk, lemon zest, and ⅛ teaspoon pepper together in another bowl. 4. Pat the cod dry with paper towels and season with salt and pepper. Arrange the fillets, skinned-side down, on plate and brush tops evenly with mayonnaise mixture. (Tuck thinner tail ends of fillets under themselves as needed to create uniform pieces.) Working with 1 fillet at a time, dredge the coated side in panko mixture, pressing gently to adhere. Arrange the fillets, crumb-side up, on sling in the prepared basket, spaced evenly apart. 5. Bake for 12 to 16 minutes, using a sling to rotate fillets halfway through cooking. Using a sling, carefully remove cod from air fryer. Serve with the lemon wedges.

Oyster Po'Boy

Prep time: 20 minutes | Cook time: 5 minutes | Serves 4

55 g plain flour
20 g yellow cornmeal
1 tablespoon Cajun seasoning
1 teaspoon salt
2 large eggs, beaten
1 teaspoon hot sauce
455 g pre-shucked oysters
1 (12-inch) French baguette, quartered and sliced horizontally
Tartar Sauce, as needed
150 g shredded lettuce, divided
2 tomatoes, cut into slices
Cooking spray

1. In a shallow bowl, whisk the flour, cornmeal, Cajun seasoning, and salt until blended. In a second shallow bowl, whisk together the eggs and hot sauce. 2. One at a time, dip the oysters in the cornmeal mixture, the eggs, and again in the cornmeal, coating thoroughly. 3. Preheat the air fryer to 200ºC. Line one of the air fryer baskets with baking paper. 4. Place the oysters on the baking paper and spritz with oil. 5. Air fry for 2 minutes. Shake the basket, spritz the oysters with oil, and air fry for 3 minutes more until lightly browned and crispy. 6. Spread each sandwich half with Tartar Sauce. Assemble the po'boys by layering each sandwich with fried oysters, ½ cup shredded lettuce, and 2 tomato slices. 7. Serve immediately.

Lemon Mahi-Mahi & Sweet Tilapia Fillets

Prep time: 10 minutes | Cook time: 14 minutes

Lemon Mahi-Mahi | Serves 2:
Olive or vegetable oil, for spraying
2 (170 g) dolphinfish
1 tablespoon lemon juice
1 tablespoon olive oil
¼ teaspoon salt
¼ teaspoon freshly ground black pepper
1 tablespoon chopped fresh dill
2 lemon slices
Sweet Tilapia Fillets | Serves 4:
2 tablespoons granulated sweetener
1 tablespoon apple cider vinegar
4 tilapia fillets, boneless
1 teaspoon olive oil

Prepare for Lemon Mahi-Mahi:
1. Line zone 1 with baking paper and spray lightly with oil.
2. Place the mahi-mahi in the prepared basket.
3. In a small bowl, whisk together the lemon juice and olive oil. Brush the mixture evenly over the mahi-mahi.
4. Sprinkle the mahi-mahi with the salt and black pepper and top with the dill.
Prepare for Sweet Tilapia Fillets:
1. Mix apple cider vinegar with olive oil and sweetener.
2. Then rub the tilapia fillets with the sweet mixture and put in zone 2 basket in one layer.
Cook:
1. In zone 1, adjust the air fryer temperature to 200ºC and air fry for 12 to 14 minutes.
2. In zone 2, adjust the air fryer temperature to 180ºC and air fry for 7 minutes per side.
3. Press SYNC, then press Start.
4. For zone 1, transfer to plates, top each with a lemon slice, and serve.

Cayenne Sole Cutlets & Almond-Crusted Fish

Prep time: 30 minutes | Cook time: 10 minutes

Cayenne Sole Cutlets | Serves 2:
1 egg
120 g Pecorino Romano cheese, grated
Sea salt and white pepper, to taste
½ teaspoon cayenne pepper
1 teaspoon dried parsley flakes
2 sole fillets
Almond-Crusted Fish | Serves 4:
4 firm white fish fillets, 110g

each
25 g breadcrumbs
20 g slivered almonds, crushed
2 tablespoons lemon juice
⅛ teaspoon cayenne
Salt and pepper, to taste
470 g plain flour
1 egg, beaten with 1 tablespoon water
Olive or vegetable oil for misting or cooking spray

Prepare for Cayenne Sole Cutlets:
1. To make a breading station, whisk the egg until frothy.
2. In another bowl, mix Pecorino Romano cheese, and spices.
3. Dip the fish in the egg mixture and turn to coat evenly; then, dredge in the cracker crumb mixture, turning a couple of times to coat evenly.
4. Cook in zone 1.
Prepare for Almond-Crusted Fish:
1. Split fish fillets lengthwise down the center to create 8 pieces.
2. Mix breadcrumbs and almonds together and set aside.
3. Mix the lemon juice and cayenne together. Brush on all sides of fish.
4. Season fish to taste with salt and pepper.
5. Place the flour on a sheet of wax paper.
6. Roll fillets in flour, dip in egg wash, and roll in the crumb mixture.
7. Mist both sides of fish with oil or cooking spray.
8. Spray zone 2 drawer and lay fillets inside.
Cook:
1. In zone 1, adjust the air fryer temperature to 200°C and air fry for 5 minutes.
2. In zone 2, adjust the air fryer temperature to 200°C and air fry for 5 minutes.
3. Press SYNC, then press Start.
4. For zone 1, turn them over and cook another 5 minutes. Enjoy!
5. For zone 2, turn fish over, and cook for an additional 5 minutes or until fish is done and flakes easily.

Panko-Crusted Fish Sticks

Prep time: 10 minutes | Cook time: 15 minutes | Serves 4

Tartar Sauce:
470 ml mayonnaise
2 tablespoons dill pickle relish
1 tablespoon dried minced onions
Fish Sticks:
Olive or vegetable oil, for spraying
455 g tilapia fillets

40 g plain flour
60 g panko bread crumbs
2 tablespoons Creole seasoning
2 teaspoons garlic granules
1 teaspoon onion powder
½ teaspoon salt
¼ teaspoon freshly ground black pepper
1 large egg

Make the Tartar Sauce: 1. In a small bowl, whisk together the mayonnaise, pickle relish, and onions. Cover with plastic wrap and refrigerate until ready to serve. You can make this sauce ahead of time; the flavours will intensify as it chills. Make the Fish Sticks: 2. Preheat the air fryer to 180°C. Line one of the air fryer baskets with baking paper and spray lightly with oil. 3. Cut the fillets into equal-size sticks and place them in a zip-top plastic bag. 4. Add the flour to the bag, seal, and shake well until evenly coated. 5. In a shallow bowl, mix together the bread crumbs, Creole seasoning, garlic, onion powder, salt, and black pepper. 6. In a small bowl, whisk the egg. 7. Dip the fish sticks in the egg, then dredge in the bread crumb mixture until completely coated. 8. Place the fish sticks in the prepared basket. You may need to work in batches, depending on the size of your air fryer. Do not overcrowd. Spray lightly with oil. 9. Cook for 12 to 15 minutes, or until browned and cooked through. Serve with the tartar sauce.

Chapter 6 Snacks and Appetizers

Chapter 6 Snacks and Appetizers

Sweet Potato Fries with Mayonnaise

Prep time: 5 minutes | Cook time: 20 minutes | Serves 2 to 3

1 large sweet potato (about 450 g), scrubbed	60 ml light mayonnaise
1 teaspoon mixed vegetables or rapeseed oil	½ teaspoon sriracha sauce
Salt, to taste	1 tablespoon spicy brown mustard
Dipping Sauce:	1 tablespoon sweet Thai chilli sauce

1. Preheat the air fryer to 90ºC. 2. On a flat work surface, cut the sweet potato into fry-shaped strips about ¼ inch wide and ¼ inch thick. You can use a mandoline to slice the sweet potato quickly and uniformly. 3. In a medium-sized bowl, drizzle the sweet potato strips with the oil and toss well. 4. Transfer to one of the air fryer baskets and air fry for 10 minutes, shaking the basket twice during cooking. 5. Remove one of the air fryer baskets and sprinkle with the salt and toss to coat. 6. Increase the air fryer temperature to 200ºC and air fry for an additional 10 minutes, or until the fries are crispy and tender. Shake the basket a few times during cooking. 7. Meanwhile, whisk together all the ingredients for the sauce in a small bowl. 8. Remove the sweet potato fries from the basket to a plate and serve warm alongside the dipping sauce.

Skinny Fries

Prep time: 10 minutes | Cook time: 15 minutes per batch | Serves 2

2 to 3 russet potatoes or Maris Piper potatoes, peeled and cut into ¼-inch sticks	2 to 3 teaspoons olive or mixed vegetables oil
	Salt, to taste

1. Cut the potatoes into ¼-inch strips. (A mandolin with a julienne blade is really helpful here.) Rinse the potatoes with cold water several times and let them soak in cold water for at least 10 minutes or as long as overnight. 2. Preheat the air fryer to 190ºC. 3. Drain and dry the potato sticks really well, using a clean kitchen towel. Toss the fries with the oil in a bowl and then air fry the fries in two batches at 190ºC for 15 minutes, shaking the basket a couple of times while they cook. 4. Add the first batch of chips back into one of the air fryer baskets with the finishing batch and let everything warm through for a few minutes. As soon as the fries are done, season them with salt and transfer to a plate or basket. Serve them warm with tomato ketchup or your favourite dip.

Sweet Bacon Potato Crunchies & Poutine with Waffle Fries

Prep time: 15 minutes | Cook time: 17 minutes

Sweet Bacon Potato Crunchies | Serves 4:	Serves 4:
24 frozen potato crisps	225 g frozen waffle cut fries
6 slices cooked bacon	2 teaspoons olive oil
2 tablespoons maple syrup	1 red pepper, chopped
110 g shredded Cheddar cheese	2 spring onions, sliced
Poutine with Waffle Fries |	90 g shredded Swiss cheese
	120 ml bottled chicken gravy

Prepare for Sweet Bacon Potato Crunchies:
1. Preheat the air fryer to 200ºC.
2. Put the potato crisps in zone 1.
3. Cut the bacon into 1-inch pieces.
Prepare for Poutine with Waffle Fries:
1. Preheat the air fryer to 190ºC.
2. Toss the waffle fries with the olive oil and place in zone 2.
Cook:
1. In zone 1, adjust the air fryer temperature to 200ºC and air fry for 10 minutes, or until the fries are crisp and light golden.
2. In zone 2, adjust the air fryer temperature to 190ºC and air fry for 12 minutes.
3. Press SYNC, then press Start.
4. For zone 1, shaking the basket halfway through the cooking time. Remove the potato crisps from the air fryer basket and put into a baking pan. Top with the bacon and drizzle with the maple syrup. Air fry for 5 minutes, or until the crunchies and bacon are crisp. Top with the cheese and air fry for 2 minutes, or until the cheese is melted. Serve hot.
5. For zone 2, shaking the basket halfway through the cooking time. Transfer the fries to a baking pan and top with the pepper, spring onions, and cheese. Air fry for 3 minutes, or until the mixed vegetables are crisp and tender. Remove the pan from the air fryer and drizzle the gravy over the fries. Air fry for 2 minutes, or until the gravy is hot. Serve immediately.

Egg Roll Pizza Sticks

Prep time: 10 minutes | Cook time: 5 minutes |
Serves 4

Olive oil
8 pieces low-fat string cheese
8 egg roll wrappers or spring roll pastry

24 slices turkey pepperoni or salami
Marinara sauce, for dipping (optional)

1. Spray one of the air fryer baskets lightly with olive oil. Fill a small bowl with water. 2. Place each egg roll wrapper diagonally on a work surface. It should look like a diamond. 3. Place 3 slices of turkey pepperoni in a vertical line down the centre of the wrapper. 4. Place 1 mozzarella cheese cheese stick on top of the turkey pepperoni. 5. Fold the top and bottom corners of the egg roll wrapper over the cheese stick. 6. Fold the left corner over the cheese stick and roll the cheese stick up to resemble a spring roll. Dip a finger in the water and seal the edge of the roll 7. Repeat with the rest of the pizza sticks. 8. Place them in one of the air fryer baskets in a single layer, making sure to leave a little space between each one. Lightly spray the pizza sticks with oil. You may need to cook these in batches. 9. Air fry at 190ºC until the pizza sticks are lightly browned and crispy, about 5 minutes. 10. These are best served hot while the cheese is melted. Accompany with a small bowl of marinara sauce, if desired.

Onion Pakoras

Prep time: 30 minutes | Cook time: 10 minutes per
batch | Serves 2

two medium-sized brown or white onions, sliced (475 g)
30 g finely chopped fresh coriander
2 tablespoons mixed vegetables oil
1 tablespoon gram flour

1 tablespoon rice flour, or 2 tablespoons gram flour
1 teaspoon turmeric powder
1 teaspoon cumin seeds
1 teaspoon rock salt
½ teaspoon cayenne pepper
mixed vegetables oil spray

1. 1.In a large bowl, combine the onions, coriander, oil, gram flour, rice flour, turmeric, cumin seeds, salt, and cayenne. Stir to combine. Cover and let stand for 30 minutes or up to overnight. (This allows the onions to release moisture, creating a batter.) Mix well before using. 2. Spray one of the air fryer baskets generously with mixed vegetables oil spray. Drop half of the batter in 6 heaped tablespoons into the basket. Set the air fryer to 180ºC for 8 minutes. Carefully turn the pakoras over and spray with oil spray. Set the air fryer for 2 minutes, or until the batter is fully cooked and crisp. 3. Repeat with remaining batter to make 6 more pakoras, checking at 6 minutes for degree of doneness. Serve hot.

Cheesy Courgette Tots

Prep time: 15 minutes | Cook time: 6 minutes |
Serves 8

2 medium courgette (about 340 g), shredded
1 large egg, whisked
72 g grated pecorino Romano cheese

42 g panko breadcrumbs
¼ teaspoon black pepper
1 clove garlic, minced
Cooking spray

1. Using your hands, squeeze out as much liquid from the courgette as possible. In a large bowl, mix the courgette with the remaining ingredients except the oil until well incorporated. 2. Make the courgette tots: Use a spoon or cookie scoop to place tablespoonfuls of the courgette mixture onto a lightly floured cutting board and form into 1-inch logs. 3. Preheat air fryer to 190ºC. Spritz the air fryer baskets with cooking spray. 4. Place the tots in 2 baskets. You may need to cook in batches to avoid overcrowding. 5. Air fry for 6 minutes until golden. 6. Remove from the basket to a serving plate and repeat with the remaining courgette tots. 7. Serve immediately.

Prawns Toasts with Sesame Seeds

Prep time: 15 minutes | Cook time: 6 to 8 minutes |
Serves 4 to 6

230 g raw prawns, peeled and deveined
1 egg, beaten
2 spring onions, chopped, plus more for garnish
2 tablespoons finely chopped fresh coriander
2 teaspoons grated fresh ginger

1 to 2 teaspoons sriracha sauce
1 teaspoon soy sauce
½ teaspoon toasted sesame oil
6 slices thinly sliced white sandwich bread
75 g sesame seeds
Cooking spray
Thai chilli sauce, for serving

1. Preheat the air fryer to 200ºC. Spritz the air fryer basket with cooking spray. 2. In a food processor, add the prawns, egg, spring onions, coriander, ginger, sriracha sauce, soy sauce and sesame oil, and pulse until chopped finely. You'll need to stop the food processor occasionally to scrape down the sides. Transfer the prawns mixture to a bowl. 3. On a clean work surface, cut the crusts off the sandwich bread. Using a brush, generously brush one side of each slice of bread with prawns mixture. 4. Place the sesame seeds on a plate. Press bread slices, prawns-side down, into sesame seeds to coat evenly. Cut each slice diagonally into quarters. 5. Spread the coated slices in a single layer in the air fryer basket. 6. Air fry in batches for 6 to 8 minutes, or until golden and crispy. Flip the bread slices halfway through. Repeat with the remaining bread slices. 7. Transfer to a plate and let cool for 5 minutes. Top with the chopped spring onions and serve warm with Thai chilli sauce.

Shishito Peppers with Herb Dressing

Prep time: 10 minutes | Cook time: 6 minutes |
Serves 2 to 4

170 g shishito or Padron peppers
1 tablespoon mixed vegetables oil
Rock salt and freshly ground black pepper, to taste
120 ml mayonnaise
2 tablespoons finely chopped fresh basil leaves

2 tablespoons finely chopped fresh flat-leaf parsley parsley
1 tablespoon finely chopped fresh tarragon
1 tablespoon finely finely chopped fresh chives
Finely grated zest of ½ lemon
1 tablespoon fresh lemon juice
Flaky sea salt, for serving

1. Preheat the air fryer to 200°C. 2. In a bowl, toss together the shishitos and oil to evenly coat and season with rock salt and black pepper. Transfer to the air fryer and air fry for 6 minutes, shaking the basket halfway through, or until the shishitos are blistered and lightly charred. 3. Meanwhile, in a small bowl, whisk together the mayonnaise, basil, parsley, tarragon, chives, lemon zest, and lemon juice. 4. Pile the peppers on a plate, sprinkle with flaky sea salt, and serve hot with the dressing.

Italian Rice Balls

Prep time: 20 minutes | Cook time: 10 minutes |
Makes 8 rice balls

355 g cooked sticky rice
½ teaspoon Italian seasoning blend
¾ teaspoon salt, divided
8 black olives, pitted
28 g mozzarella cheese cheese,

cut into tiny pieces (small enough to stuff into olives)
2 eggs
35 g Italian breadcrumbs
55 g panko breadcrumbs
Cooking spray

1. Preheat air fryer to 200°C. 2. Stuff each black olive with a piece of mozzarella cheese cheese. Set aside. 3. In a bowl, combine the cooked sticky rice, Italian seasoning blend, and ½ teaspoon of salt and stir to mix well. Form the rice mixture into a log with your hands and divide it into 8 equal portions. Mould each portion around a black olive and roll into a ball. 4. Transfer to the freezer to chill for 10 to 15 minutes until firm. 5. In a shallow dish, place the Italian breadcrumbs. In a separate shallow dish, whisk the eggs. In a third shallow dish, combine the panko breadcrumbs and remaining salt. 6. One by one, roll the rice balls in the Italian breadcrumbs, then dip in the whisked eggs, finally coat them with the panko breadcrumbs. 7. Arrange the rice balls in one of the air fryer baskets and spritz both sides with cooking spray. 8. Air fry for 10 minutes until the rice balls are golden. Flip the balls halfway through the cooking time. 9. Serve warm.

String Bean Fries

Prep time: 15 minutes | Cook time: 5 to 6 minutes |
Serves 4

227 g fresh French beans
2 eggs
4 teaspoons water
60 g plain flour
50 g breadcrumbs
¼ teaspoon salt

¼ teaspoon ground black pepper
¼ teaspoon mustard powder (optional)
Oil for misting or cooking spray

1. Preheat the air fryer to 180°C. 2. Trim stem ends from French beans, wash, and pat dry. 3. In a shallow dish, beat eggs and water together until well blended. 4. Place flour in a second shallow dish. 5. In a third shallow dish, stir together the breadcrumbs, salt, pepper, and mustard powder if using. 6. Dip each bean in egg mixture, flour, egg mixture again, then breadcrumbs. 7. When you finish coating all the French beans, open air fryer and place them in basket. 8. Cook for 3 minutes. 9. Stop and mist French beans with oil or cooking spray. 10. Cook for 2 to 3 more minutes or until French beans are crispy and nicely browned.

Hush Puppies

Prep time: 45 minutes | Cook time: 10 minutes |
Serves 12

144 g self-raising yellow cornmeal
60 g plain flour
1 teaspoon sugar
1 teaspoon salt
1 teaspoon freshly ground black pepper

1 large egg
80 g canned creamed sweetcorn
216 g minced onion
2 teaspoons minced jalapeño chillies pepper
2 tablespoons olive oil, divided

1. Thoroughly combine the cornmeal, flour, sugar, salt, and pepper in a large bowl. 2. Whisk together the egg and sweetcorn in a small bowl. Pour the egg mixture into the bowl of cornmeal mixture and stir to combine. Stir in the minced onion and jalapeño chillies. Cover the bowl with plastic wrap and place in the refrigerator for 30 minutes. 3. Preheat the air fryer to 190°C. Line the air fryer basket with baking paper paper and lightly brush it with 1 tablespoon of olive oil. 4. Scoop out the cornmeal mixture and form into 24 balls, about 1 inch. 5. Place them half in zone 1, the remaining in zone 2, leaving space between each ball.. In zone 1, select Air Fry button, set the time to 5 minutes. In zone 2, select Match Cook and then press Start. 6. If necessary, work in batches. Shake the basket and brush the balls with the remaining 1 tablespoon of olive oil. Continue cooking for 5 minutes until golden. 7. Remove the balls (hush puppies) from the basket and serve on a plate.

Stuffed Figs with Goat Cheese and Honey

Prep time: 5 minutes | Cook time: 10 minutes |
Serves 4

8 fresh figs
57 g goat cheese
¼ teaspoon cinnamon powder

1 tablespoon honey, plus more
for serving
1 tablespoon olive oil

1. Preheat the air fryer to 180ºC. Line an 8-by-8-inch baking dish with baking paper paper that comes up the side so you can lift it out after cooking. 2. In a large bowl, mix together all of the ingredients until well combined. 3. Press the oat mixture into the pan in an even layer. 4. Place the pan into one of the air fryer baskets and bake for 15 minutes. 5. Remove the pan from the air fryer and lift the granola cake out of the pan using the edges of the baking paper paper. 6. Allow to cool for 5 minutes before slicing into 6 equal bars. 7. Serve immediately or wrap in plastic wrap and store at room temperature for up to 1 week.

Courgette Fries with Roasted Garlic Aioli

Prep time: 20 minutes | Cook time: 12 minutes |
Serves 4

1 tablespoon mixed vegetables
oil
½ head green or savoy cabbage,
finely shredded
Roasted Garlic Aioli:
1 teaspoon roasted garlic
120 ml mayonnaise
2 tablespoons olive oil
Juice of ½ lemon

Salt and pepper, to taste
courgette fries:
64 g flour
2 eggs, beaten
72 g seasoned breadcrumbs
Salt and pepper, to taste
1 large courgette, cut into
½-inch sticks
Olive oil

1. Make the Aioli: Combine the roasted garlic, mayonnaise, olive oil and lemon juice in a bowl and whisk well. Season the Aioli with salt and pepper to taste. 2. Prepare the courgette fries. Create a dredging station with three shallow dishes. Place the flour in the first shallow dish and season well with salt and freshly ground black pepper. Put the beaten eggs in the second shallow dish. In the third shallow dish, combine the breadcrumbs, salt and pepper. Dredge the courgette sticks, coating with flour first, then dipping them into the eggs to coat, and finally tossing in breadcrumbs. Shake the dish with the breadcrumbs and pat the crumbs onto the courgette sticks gently with your hands, so they stick evenly. 3. Place the courgette fries on a flat surface and let them sit at least 10 minutes before air frying to let them dry out a little. Preheat the air fryer to 200ºC. 4.

Spray the courgette sticks with olive oil and place them into one of the air fryer baskets. You can air fry the courgette in two layers, placing the second layer in the opposite direction to the first. Air fry for 12 minutes turning and rotating the fries halfway through the cooking time. Spray with additional oil when you turn them over. 5. Serve courgette fries warm with the roasted garlic Aioli.

Lemon-Pepper Chicken Chicken Drumsticks

Prep time: 30 minutes | Cook time: 30 minutes |
Serves 2

2 teaspoons freshly ground
coarse black pepper
1 teaspoon baking powder
½ teaspoon garlic powder

4 chicken drumsticks (113 g
each)
Rock salt, to taste
1 lemon

1. In a small bowl, stir together the pepper, baking powder, and garlic powder. Place the drumsticks on a plate and sprinkle evenly with the baking powder mixture, turning the drumsticks so they're well coated. Let the drumsticks stand in the refrigerator for at least 1 hour or up to overnight. 2. Sprinkle the drumsticks with salt, then transfer them to the air fryer, standing them bone-side up and leaning against the wall of one of the air fryer baskets. Air fry at 190ºC until fully cooked and crisp on the outside, about 30 minutes. 3. Transfer the drumsticks to a serving platter and finely grate the lemon zest over them while they're hot. Cut the lemon into wedges and serve with the warm drumsticks.

Sea Salt Potato Crisps

Prep time: 30 minutes | Cook time: 27 minutes |
Serves 4

Oil, for spraying
4 medium-sized yellow potatoes
such as Maris Piper potatoes

1 tablespoon oil
⅛ to ¼ teaspoon fine sea salt

1. Line one of the air fryer baskets with baking paper and spray lightly with oil. 2. Using a mandoline or a very sharp knife, cut the potatoes into very thin slices. 3. Place the slices in a bowl of cold water and let soak for about 20 minutes. 4. Drain the potatoes, transfer them to a plate lined with kitchen roll, and pat dry. 5. Drizzle the oil over the potatoes, sprinkle with the salt, and toss to combine. Transfer to the prepared basket. 6. Air fry at 90ºC for 20 minutes. Toss the crisps, increase the heat to 200ºC, and cook for another 5 to 7 minutes, until crispy.

Kale Chips with Tex-Mex Dip

Prep time: 10 minutes | Cook time: 5 to 6 minutes |
Serves 8

240 ml Greek yoghurt	1 bunch curly kale
1 tablespoon chili powder	1 teaspoon olive oil
80 ml low-salt salsa, well drained	¼ teaspoon coarse sea salt

1. In a small bowl, combine the yoghurt, chili powder, and drained salsa; refrigerate. 2. Rinse the kale thoroughly, and pat dry. Remove the stems and ribs from the kale, using a sharp knife. Cut or tear the leaves into 3-inch pieces. 3. Toss the kale with the olive oil in a large bowl. 4. Air fry the kale in small batches at 200ºC until the leaves are crisp. This should take 5 to 6 minutes. Shake the basket once during cooking time. 5. As you remove the kale chips, sprinkle them with a bit of the sea salt. 6. When all of the kale chips are done, serve with the dip.

Jalapeño Poppers & Crispy Breaded Beef Cubes

Prep time: 20 minutes | Cook time: 20 minutes

Jalapeño Poppers	Serves 4:	seeded
Oil, for spraying	Crispy Breaded Beef Cubes	
227 g soft white cheese	Serves 4:
177 ml gluten-free breadcrumbs, divided	450 g sirloin tip, cut into 1-inch cubes
2 tablespoons chopped fresh parsley	240 ml cheese pasta sauce
½ teaspoon granulated garlic	355 g soft breadcrumbs
½ teaspoon salt	2 tablespoons olive oil
10 jalapeño peppers, halved and	½ teaspoon dried marjoram

Prepare for Jalapeño Poppers:
1. Line zone 1 basket with parchment and spray lightly with oil.
2. In a medium bowl, mix together the soft white cheese, half of the breadcrumbs, the parsley, garlic, and salt.
3. Spoon the mixture into the jalapeño halves. Gently press the stuffed jalapeños in the remaining breadcrumbs.
4. Place the stuffed jalapeños in the prepared basket.
Prepare for Crispy Breaded Beef Cubes:
1. Preheat the air fryer to 180ºC.
2. In a medium-sized bowl, toss the beef with the pasta sauce to coat.
3. In a shallow dish, combine the breadcrumbs, oil, and marjoram, and mix well. Drop the beef cubes, one at a time, into the bread crumb mixture to coat thoroughly.
4. Put in zone 2. If necessary, work in batches.

Cook:
1. In zone 1, adjust the air fryer temperature to 190ºC and air fry for 20 minutes, or until the cheese is melted and the breadcrumbs are crisp and golden brown.
2. In zone 2, adjust the air fryer temperature to 170ºC and air fry for 6 to 8 minutes.
3. Press SYNC, then press Start.
4. For zone 2, shaking the basket once during cooking time, until the beef is at least 63ºC and the outside is crisp and brown.

Artichoke and Olive Pitta Flatbread

Prep time: 5 minutes | Cook time: 10 minutes |
Serves 4

2 wholewheat pitta bread	70 g Kalamata olives
2 tablespoons olive oil, divided	30 g shredded Parmesan
2 garlic cloves, minced	55 g crumbled feta cheese
¼ teaspoon salt	Chopped fresh parsley, for garnish (optional)
120 g canned artichoke hearts, sliced	

1. Preheat the air fryer to 190ºC. 2. Brush each pitta with 1 tablespoon olive oil, then sprinkle the minced garlic and salt over the top. 3. Distribute the artichoke hearts, olives, and cheeses evenly between the two pitta bread, and place both into the air fryer to bake for 10 minutes. 4. Remove the pitta bread and cut them into 4 pieces each before serving. Sprinkle parsley over the top, if desired.

Spinach and Crab Meat Cups

Prep time: 10 minutes | Cook time: 10 minutes |
Makes 30 cups

1 (170 g) can crab meat, drained to yield 80 g meat	¼ teaspoon lemon juice
30 g frozen spinach, thawed, drained, and chopped	½ teaspoon Worcestershire sauce
1 clove garlic, minced	30 mini frozen filo shells, thawed
84 g grated Parmesan cheese	Cooking spray
3 tablespoons plain yoghurt	

1. Preheat the air fryer to 200ºC. 2. Remove any bits of shell that might remain in the crab meat. 3. Mix the crab meat, spinach, garlic, and cheese together. 4. Stir in the yoghurt, lemon juice, and Worcestershire sauce and mix well. 5. Spoon a teaspoon of filling into each filo shell. 6. Spray the air fryer baskets with cooking spray and arrange half the shells in zone 1, the remaining in zone 2. Air fry for 5 minutes. Repeat with the remaining shells. 7. Serve immediately.

Chilli-brined Fried Calamari

Prep time: 20 minutes | Cook time: 8 minutes | Serves 2

1 (227 g) jar sweet or hot pickled cherry peppers
227 g calamari bodies and tentacles, bodies cut into ½-inch-wide rings
1 lemon
200 g plain flour
Rock salt and freshly ground

black pepper, to taste
3 large eggs, lightly beaten
Cooking spray
120 ml mayonnaise
1 teaspoon finely chopped rosemary
1 garlic clove, minced

1. Drain the pickled pepper brine into a large bowl and tear the peppers into bite-size strips. Add the pepper strips and calamari to the brine and let stand in the refrigerator for 20 minutes or up to 2 hours. 2. Grate the lemon zest into a large bowl then whisk in the flour and season with salt and pepper. Dip the calamari and pepper strips in the egg, then toss them in the flour mixture until fully coated. Spray the calamari and peppers liberally with cooking spray, then transfer half to the air fryer. Air fry at 200℃, shaking the basket halfway into cooking, until the calamari is fully cooked and golden, about 8 minutes. Transfer to a plate and repeat with the remaining pieces. 3. In a small bowl, whisk together the mayonnaise, rosemary, and garlic. Squeeze half the zested lemon to get 1 tablespoon of juice and stir it into the sauce. Season with salt and pepper. Cut the remaining zested lemon half into 4 small wedges and serve alongside the calamari, peppers, and sauce.

Crispy Green Tomatoes with Horseradish

Prep time: 18 minutes | Cook time: 10 to 15 minutes | Serves 4

2 eggs
60 ml buttermilk
55 g breadcrumbs
75 g cornmeal
¼ teaspoon salt
680 g firm green tomatoes, cut into ¼-inch slices
Cooking spray
Horseradish Sauce:

60 ml soured cream
60 ml mayonnaise
2 teaspoons prepared horseradish
½ teaspoon lemon juice
½ teaspoon Worcestershire sauce
⅛ teaspoon black pepper

1. Preheat air fryer to 200℃. Spritz one of the air fryer baskets with cooking spray. 2. In a small bowl, whisk together all the ingredients for the horseradish sauce until smooth. Set aside. 3. In a shallow dish, beat the eggs and buttermilk. 4. In a separate shallow dish, thoroughly combine the breadcrumbs, cornmeal, and salt. 5.

Dredge the tomato slices, one at a time, in the egg mixture, then roll in the bread crumb mixture until evenly coated. 6. Working in batches, place the tomato slices in one of the air fryer baskets in a single layer. Spray them with cooking spray. 7. Air fry for 10 to 15 minutes, flipping the slices halfway through, or until the tomato slices are nicely browned and crisp. 8. Remove from the basket to a platter and repeat with the remaining tomato slices. 9. Serve drizzled with the prepared horseradish sauce.

Browned Ricotta with Capers and Lemon

Prep time: 10 minutes | Cook time: 8 to 10 minutes | Serves 4 to 6

320 g whole milk ricotta cheese
2 tablespoons extra-virgin olive oil
2 tablespoons capers, rinsed
Zest of 1 lemon, plus more for garnish
1 teaspoon finely chopped fresh

rosemary
Pinch crushed red pepper flakes
Salt and freshly ground black pepper, to taste
1 tablespoon grated Parmesan cheese

1. Preheat the air fryer to 190℃. 2. In a mixing bowl, stir together the ricotta cheese, olive oil, capers, lemon zest, rosemary, red pepper flakes, salt, and pepper until well combined. 3. Spread the mixture evenly in a baking dish and place it in one of the air fryer baskets. 4. Air fry for 8 to 10 minutes until the top is nicely browned. 5. Remove from the basket and top with a sprinkle of grated Parmesan cheese. 6. Garnish with the lemon zest and serve warm.

Crunchy Tex-Mex Tortilla Chips

Prep time: 5 minutes | Cook time: 5 minutes | Serves 4

Olive oil
½ teaspoon salt
½ teaspoon cumin powder
½ teaspoon chili powder

½ teaspoon paprika
Pinch cayenne pepper
8 (6-inch) sweetcorn tortillas, each cut into 6 wedges

1. Spray fryer basket lightly with olive oil. 2. In a small bowl, combine the salt, cumin, chili powder, paprika, and cayenne pepper. 3. Place the tortilla wedges in one of the air fryer baskets in a single layer. Spray the tortillas lightly with oil and sprinkle with some of the seasoning mixture. You will need to cook the tortillas in batches. 4. Air fry at 190℃ for 2 to 3 minutes. Shake the basket and cook until the chips are light brown and crispy, an additional 2 to 3 minutes. Watch the chips closely so they do not burn.

Chapter 7 Vegetables and Sides

Chapter 7 Vegetables and Sides

Green Tomato Salad

Prep time: 10 minutes | Cook time: 8 to 10 minutes | Serves 4

4 green tomatoes	2 teaspoons fresh lemon juice
½ teaspoon salt	2 tablespoons finely chopped
1 large egg, lightly beaten	fresh parsley
50 g peanut flour	1 teaspoon dried dill
1 tablespoon Creole seasoning	1 teaspoon dried chives
1 (140 g) bag rocket	½ teaspoon salt
Buttermilk Dressing:	½ teaspoon garlic powder
230 g mayonnaise	½ teaspoon onion powder
120 g sour cream	

1. Preheat the air fryer to 200ºC. 2. Slice the tomatoes into ½-inch slices and sprinkle with the salt. Let sit for 5 to 10 minutes. 3. Place the egg in a small shallow bowl. In another small shallow bowl, combine the peanut flour and Creole seasoning. Dip each tomato slice into the egg wash, then dip into the peanut flour mixture, turning to coat evenly. 4. Working in batches if necessary, arrange the tomato slices in a single layer in one of the air fryer baskets and spray both sides lightly with olive oil. Air fry until browned and crisp, 8 to 10 minutes. 5. To make the buttermilk dressing: In a small bowl, whisk together the mayonnaise, sour cream, lemon juice, parsley, dill, chives, salt, garlic powder, and onion powder. 6. Serve the tomato slices on top of a bed of the rocket with the dressing on the side.

Breaded Green Tomatoes

Prep time: 15 minutes | Cook time: 30 minutes | Serves 4

60 g plain flour	Salt and freshly ground black
2 eggs	pepper, to taste
60 g semolina	2 green tomatoes, cut into
60 g panko bread crumbs	½-inch-thick rounds
1 teaspoon garlic powder	Cooking oil spray

1. Place the flour in a small bowl. 2. In another small bowl, beat the eggs. 3. In a third small bowl, stir together the semolina, panko, and garlic powder. Season with salt and pepper. 4. Dip each tomato slice into the flour, the egg, and finally the semolina mixture to coat. 5. Insert the crisper plate into the basket and the basket into the unit. Preheat the unit by selecting AIR FRY, setting the temperature to 200ºC, and setting the time to 3 minutes. Select START/STOP to begin. 6. Once the unit is preheated, spray the crisper plate and the basket with cooking oil. Working in batches, place the tomato slices in the air fryer in a single layer. Do not stack them. Spray the tomato slices with the cooking oil. 7. Select AIR FRY, set the temperature to 200ºC, and set the time to 10 minutes. Select START/STOP to begin. 8. After 5 minutes, use tongs to flip the tomatoes. Resume cooking for 4 to 5 minutes, or until crisp. 9. When the cooking is complete, transfer the fried green tomatoes to a plate. Repeat steps 6, 7, and 8 for the remaining tomatoes.

Broccoli-Cheddar Twice-Baked Potatoes

Prep time: 10 minutes | Cook time: 46 minutes | Serves 4

Oil, for spraying	1 tablespoon sour cream
2 medium Maris Piper potatoes	1 teaspoon garlic powder
1 tablespoon olive oil	1 teaspoon onion powder
30 g broccoli florets	60 g shredded Cheddar cheese

1. Line one of the air fryer baskets with parchment and spray lightly with oil. 2. Rinse the potatoes and pat dry with paper towels. Rub the outside of the potatoes with the olive oil and place them in the prepared basket. 3. Air fry at 200ºC for 40 minutes, or until easily pierced with a fork. Let cool just enough to handle, then cut the potatoes in half lengthwise. 4. Meanwhile, place the broccoli in a microwave-safe bowl, cover with water, and microwave on high for 5 to 8 minutes. Drain and set aside. 5. Scoop out most of the potato flesh and transfer to a medium bowl. 6. Add the sour cream, garlic, and onion powder and stir until the potatoes are mashed. 7. Spoon the potato mixture back into the hollowed potato skins, mounding it to fit, if necessary. Top with the broccoli and cheese. Return the potatoes to the basket. You may need to work in batches, depending on the size of your air fryer. 8. Air fry at 200ºC for 3 to 6 minutes, or until the cheese has melted. Serve immediately.

Spiced Butternut Squash

**Prep time: 10 minutes | Cook time: 15 minutes |
Serves 4**

600 g 1-inch-cubed butternut squash	1 to 2 tablespoons brown sugar
2 tablespoons vegetable oil	1 teaspoon Chinese five-spice powder

1. In a medium bowl, combine the squash, oil, sugar, and five-spice powder. Toss to coat. 2. Place the squash in one of the air fryer baskets. Set the air fryer to 200ºC for 15 minutes or until tender.

Lebanese Baba Ghanoush

**Prep time: 15 minutes | Cook time: 20 minutes |
Serves 4**

1 medium aubergine	1 tablespoon extra-virgin olive oil
2 tablespoons vegetable oil	
2 tablespoons tahini (sesame paste)	½ teaspoon smoked paprika
2 tablespoons fresh lemon juice	2 tablespoons chopped fresh parsley
½ teaspoon coarse sea salt	

1. Rub the aubergine all over with the vegetable oil. Place the aubergine in one of the air fryer baskets. Set the air fryer to 200ºC for 20 minutes, or until the aubergine skin is blistered and charred. 2. Transfer the aubergine to a re-sealable plastic bag, seal, and set aside for 15 minutes (the aubergine will finish cooking in the residual heat trapped in the bag). 3. Transfer the aubergine to a large bowl. Peel off and discard the charred skin. Roughly mash the aubergine flesh. Add the tahini, lemon juice, and salt. Stir to combine. 4. Transfer the mixture to a serving bowl. Drizzle with the olive oil. Sprinkle with the paprika and parsley and serve.

Roasted Grape Tomatoes and Asparagus

**Prep time: 5 minutes | Cook time: 12 minutes |
Serves 6**

400 g grape tomatoes	3 garlic cloves, minced
1 bunch asparagus, trimmed	½ teaspoon coarse sea salt
2 tablespoons olive oil	

1. Preheat the air fryer to 190ºC. 2. In a large bowl, combine all of the ingredients, tossing until the vegetables are well coated with oil. 3. Pour the vegetable mixture half in zone 1, the remaining in zone 2 and spread into a single layer, then roast for 12 minutes.

Garlic Roasted Broccoli

**Prep time: 8 minutes | Cook time: 10 to 14 minutes |
Serves 6**

1 head broccoli, cut into bite-size florets	Sea salt and freshly ground black pepper, to taste
1 tablespoon avocado oil	1 tablespoon freshly squeezed lemon juice
2 teaspoons minced garlic	
⅛ teaspoon red pepper flakes	½ teaspoon lemon zest

1. In a large bowl, toss together the broccoli, avocado oil, garlic, red pepper flakes, salt, and pepper. 2. Set the air fryer to 190ºC. Arrange the broccoli in a single layer half in zone 1, the remaining in zone 2, working in batches if necessary. Roast for 10 to 14 minutes, until the broccoli is lightly charred. 3. Place the florets in a medium bowl and toss with the lemon juice and lemon zest. Serve.

Hasselback Potatoes with Chive Pesto

**Prep time: 10 minutes | Cook time: 40 minutes |
Serves 2**

2 medium Maris Piper potatoes	leaf parsley leaves
5 tablespoons olive oil	1 tablespoon chopped walnuts
coarse sea salt and freshly ground black pepper, to taste	1 tablespoon grated Parmesan cheese
10 g roughly chopped fresh chives	1 teaspoon fresh lemon juice
	1 small garlic clove, peeled
2 tablespoons packed fresh flat-	60 g sour cream

1. Place the potatoes on a cutting board and lay a chopstick or thin-handled wooden spoon to the side of each potato. Thinly slice the potatoes crosswise, letting the chopstick or spoon handle stop the blade of your knife, and stop ½ inch short of each end of the potato. Rub the potatoes with 1 tablespoon of the olive oil and season with salt and pepper. 2. Place the potatoes, cut-side up, in the air fryer and air fry at 190ºC until golden brown and crisp on the outside and tender inside, about 40 minutes, drizzling the insides with 1 tablespoon more olive oil and seasoning with more salt and pepper halfway through. 3. Meanwhile, in a small blender or food processor, combine the remaining 3 tablespoons olive oil, the chives, parsley, walnuts, Parmesan, lemon juice, and garlic and purée until smooth. Season the chive pesto with salt and pepper. 4. Remove the potatoes from the air fryer and transfer to plates. Drizzle the potatoes with the pesto, letting it drip down into the grooves, then dollop each with sour cream and serve hot.

Sausage-Stuffed Mushroom Caps

Prep time: 10 minutes | Cook time: 8 minutes |
Serves 2

6 large portobello mushroom caps	2 tablespoons blanched finely ground almond flour
230 g Italian sausage	20 g grated Parmesan cheese
15 g chopped onion	1 teaspoon minced fresh garlic

1. Use a spoon to hollow out each mushroom cap, reserving scrapings. 2. In a medium skillet over medium heat, brown the sausage about 10 minutes or until fully cooked and no pink remains. Drain and then add reserved mushroom scrapings, onion, almond flour, Parmesan, and garlic. Gently fold ingredients together and continue cooking an additional minute, then remove from heat. 3. Evenly spoon the mixture into mushroom caps and place the caps into a 6-inch round pan. Place pan into one of the air fryer baskets. 4. Adjust the temperature to 190ºC and set the timer for 8 minutes. 5. When finished cooking, the tops will be browned and bubbling. Serve warm.

Mushrooms with Goat Cheese & Southwestern Roasted Corn

Prep time: 20 minutes | Cook time: 10 minutes

Mushrooms with Goat Cheese | Serves 4:	240 g thawed frozen corn kernels
3 tablespoons vegetable oil	50 g diced yellow onion
450 g mixed mushrooms, trimmed and sliced	150 g mixed diced bell peppers
1 clove garlic, minced	1 jalapeño, diced
¼ teaspoon dried thyme	1 tablespoon fresh lemon juice
½ teaspoon black pepper	1 teaspoon ground cumin
110 g goat cheese, diced	½ teaspoon ancho chili powder
2 teaspoons chopped fresh thyme leaves (optional)	½ teaspoon coarse sea salt
Southwestern Roasted Corn | Serves 4:	For Serving:
Corn:	150 g queso fresco or feta cheese
	10 g chopped fresh coriander
	1 tablespoon fresh lemon juice

Prepare for Mushrooms with Goat Cheese:
1. In a baking pan, combine the oil, mushrooms, garlic, dried thyme, and pepper. Stir in the goat cheese.
2. Place the pan in zone 1.
Prepare for Southwestern Roasted Corn:
1. For the corn: In a large bowl, stir together the corn, onion, bell peppers, jalapeño, lemon juice, cumin, chili powder, and salt until well incorporated.
2. Pour the spiced vegetables into zone 2.

Cook:
1. In zone 1, adjust the air fryer temperature to 200ºC and air fry for 10 minutes.
2. In zone 2, adjust the air fryer temperature to 190ºC and air fry for 10 minutes.
3. Press SYNC, then press Start.
4. For zone 1, stirring halfway through the cooking time. Sprinkle with fresh thyme, if desired.
5. For zone 2, stirring halfway through the cooking time. Transfer the corn mixture to a serving bowl. Add the cheese, coriander, and lemon juice and stir well to combine. Serve immediately.

Fig, Chickpea, and Rocket Salad

Prep time: 15 minutes | Cook time: 20 minutes |
Serves 4

8 fresh figs, halved	2 tablespoons extra-virgin olive oil, plus more for greasing
250 g cooked chickpeas	
1 teaspoon crushed roasted cumin seeds	Salt and ground black pepper, to taste
4 tablespoons balsamic vinegar	40 g rocket, washed and dried

1. Preheat the air fryer to 190ºC. 2. Cover one of the air fryer baskets with aluminum foil and grease lightly with oil. Put the figs in the air fryer basket and air fry for 10 minutes. 3. In a bowl, combine the chickpeas and cumin seeds. 4. Remove the air fried figs from the air fryer and replace with the chickpeas. Air fry for 10 minutes. Leave to cool. 5. In the meantime, prepare the dressing. Mix the balsamic vinegar, olive oil, salt and pepper. 6. In a salad bowl, combine the rocket with the cooled figs and chickpeas. 7. Toss with the sauce and serve.

Corn Croquettes

Prep time: 10 minutes | Cook time: 12 to 14 minutes
| Serves 4

105 g leftover mashed potatoes	pepper
340 g corn kernels (if frozen, thawed, and well drained)	¼ teaspoon salt
	50 g panko bread crumbs
¼ teaspoon onion powder	Oil for misting or cooking spray
⅛ teaspoon ground black	

1. Place the potatoes and half the corn in food processor and pulse until corn is well chopped. 2. Transfer mixture to large bowl and stir in remaining corn, onion powder, pepper and salt. 3. Shape mixture into 16 balls. 4. Roll balls in panko crumbs, mist with oil or cooking spray, and place in air fryer basket. 5. Air fry at 180ºC for 12 to 14 minutes, until golden brown and crispy.

Easy Potato Croquettes

Prep time: 15 minutes | Cook time: 15 minutes | Serves 10

55 g nutritional yeast
300 g boiled potatoes, mashed
1 flax egg
1 tablespoon flour
2 tablespoons chopped chives

Salt and ground black pepper, to taste
2 tablespoons vegetable oil
30 g bread crumbs

1. Preheat the air fryer to 200°C. 2. In a bowl, combine the nutritional yeast, potatoes, flax egg, flour, and chives. Sprinkle with salt and pepper as desired. 3. In a separate bowl, mix the vegetable oil and bread crumbs to achieve a crumbly consistency. 4. Shape the potato mixture into small balls and dip each one into the bread crumb mixture. 5. Put the croquettes half in zone 1, the remaining in zone 2 and air fry for 15 minutes, ensuring the croquettes turn golden brown. 6. Serve immediately.

Hawaiian Brown Rice

Prep time: 10 minutes | Cook time: 12 to 16 minutes | Serves 4 to 6

110 g ground sausage
1 teaspoon butter
20 g minced onion
40 g minced bell pepper

380 g cooked brown rice
1 (230 g) can crushed pineapple, drained

1. Shape sausage into 3 or 4 thin patties. Air fry at 200°C for 6 to 8 minutes or until well done. Remove from air fryer, drain, and crumble. Set aside. 2. Place butter, onion, and bell pepper in baking pan. Roast at 200°C for 1 minute and stir. Cook 3 to 4 minutes longer or just until vegetables are tender. 3. Add sausage, rice, and pineapple to vegetables and stir together. 4. Roast for 2 to 3 minutes, until heated through.

Maple-Roasted Tomatoes

Prep time: 15 minutes | Cook time: 20 minutes | Serves 2

280 g cherry tomatoes, halved
coarse sea salt, to taste
2 tablespoons maple syrup
1 tablespoon vegetable oil

2 sprigs fresh thyme, stems removed
1 garlic clove, minced
Freshly ground black pepper

1. Place the tomatoes in a colander and sprinkle liberally with salt. Let stand for 10 minutes to drain. 2. Transfer the tomatoes cut-side up to a cake pan, then drizzle with the maple syrup, followed by the oil. Sprinkle with the thyme leaves and garlic and season with pepper. Place the pan in the air fryer and roast at 160°C until the tomatoes are soft, collapsed, and lightly caramelized on top, about 20 minutes. 3. Serve straight from the pan or transfer the tomatoes to a plate and drizzle with the juices from the pan to serve.

Fried Courgette Salad

Prep time: 10 minutes | Cook time: 5 to 7 minutes | Serves 4

2 medium courgette, thinly sliced
5 tablespoons olive oil, divided
15 g chopped fresh parsley
2 tablespoons chopped fresh mint

Zest and juice of ½ lemon
1 clove garlic, minced
65 g crumbled feta cheese
Freshly ground black pepper, to taste

1. Preheat the air fryer to 200°C. 2. In a large bowl, toss the courgette slices with 1 tablespoon of the olive oil. 3. Working in batches if necessary, arrange the courgette slices in an even layer in one of the air fryer baskets. Pausing halfway through the cooking time to shake the basket, air fry for 5 to 7 minutes until soft and lightly browned on each side. 4. Meanwhile, in a small bowl, combine the remaining 4 tablespoons olive oil, parsley, mint, lemon zest, lemon juice, and garlic. 5. Arrange the courgette on a plate and drizzle with the dressing. Sprinkle the feta and black pepper on top. Serve warm or at room temperature.

Five-Spice Roasted Sweet Potatoes

Prep time: 10 minutes | Cook time: 12 minutes | Serves 4

½ teaspoon ground cinnamon
¼ teaspoon ground cumin
¼ teaspoon paprika
1 teaspoon chili powder
⅛ teaspoon turmeric
½ teaspoon salt (optional)

Freshly ground black pepper, to taste
2 large sweet potatoes, peeled and cut into ¾-inch cubes
1 tablespoon olive oil

1. In a large bowl, mix together cinnamon, cumin, paprika, chili powder, turmeric, salt, and pepper to taste. 2. Add potatoes and stir well. 3. Drizzle the seasoned potatoes with the olive oil and stir until evenly coated. 4. Place seasoned potatoes in a baking pan or an ovenproof dish that fits inside your air fryer basket. 5. Cook for 6 minutes at 200°C, stop, and stir well. 6. Cook for an additional 6 minutes.

Broccoli Tots

Prep time: 15 minutes | Cook time: 10 minutes |
Makes 24 tots

230 g broccoli florets
1 egg, beaten
⅛ teaspoon onion powder
¼ teaspoon salt
⅛ teaspoon pepper

2 tablespoons grated Parmesan
cheese
25 g panko bread crumbs
Oil for misting

1. Steam broccoli for 2 minutes. Rinse in cold water, drain well, and chop finely. 2. In a large bowl, mix broccoli with all other ingredients except the oil. 3. Scoop out small portions of mixture and shape into 24 tots. Lay them on a cookie sheet or wax paper as you work. 4. Spray tots with oil and place in air fryer basket in single layer. 5. Air fry at 200ºC for 5 minutes. Shake basket and spray with oil again. Cook 5 minutes longer or until browned and crispy.

Fried Brussels Sprouts

Prep time: 10 minutes | Cook time: 18 minutes |
Serves 4

1 teaspoon plus 1 tablespoon
extra-virgin olive oil, divided
2 teaspoons minced garlic
2 tablespoons honey
1 tablespoon sugar
2 tablespoons freshly squeezed
lemon juice
2 tablespoons rice vinegar

2 tablespoons sriracha
450 g Brussels sprouts, stems
trimmed and any tough leaves
removed, rinsed, halved
lengthwise, and dried
½ teaspoon salt
Cooking oil spray

1. In a small saucepan over low heat, combine 1 teaspoon of olive oil, the garlic, honey, sugar, lemon juice, vinegar, and sriracha. Cook for 2 to 3 minutes, or until slightly thickened. Remove the pan from the heat, cover, and set aside. 2. Place the Brussels sprouts in a resealable bag or small bowl. Add the remaining olive oil and the salt, and toss to coat. 3. Insert the crisper plate into the basket and the basket into the unit. Preheat the unit by selecting AIR FRY, setting the temperature to 200ºC, and setting the time to 3 minutes. Select START/STOP to begin. 4. Once the unit is preheated, spray the crisper plate with cooking oil. Add the Brussels sprouts to the basket. 5. Select AIR FRY, set the temperature to 200ºC, and set the time to 15 minutes. Select START/STOP to begin. 6. After 7 or 8 minutes, remove the basket and shake it to toss the sprouts. Reinsert the basket to resume cooking. 7. When the cooking is complete, the leaves should be crispy and light brown and the sprout centres tender. 8. Place the sprouts in a medium serving bowl and drizzle the sauce over the top. Toss to coat, and serve immediately.

Garlic Courgette and Red Peppers

Prep time: 5 minutes | Cook time: 15 minutes |
Serves 6

2 medium courgette, cubed
1 red pepper, diced
2 garlic cloves, sliced

2 tablespoons olive oil
½ teaspoon salt

1. Preheat the air fryer to 193ºC. 2. In a large bowl, mix together the courgette, bell pepper, and garlic with the olive oil and salt. 3. Pour the mixture half in zone 1, the remaining in zone 2, and roast for 7 minutes. Shake or stir, then roast for 7 to 8 minutes more.

"Faux-Tato" Hash

Prep time: 10 minutes | Cook time: 12 minutes |
Serves 4

450 g radishes, ends removed,
quartered
¼ medium yellow onion, peeled
and diced
½ medium green pepper, seeded
and chopped

2 tablespoons salted butter,
melted
½ teaspoon garlic powder
¼ teaspoon ground black
pepper

1. In a large bowl, combine radishes, onion, and bell pepper. Toss with butter. 2. Sprinkle garlic powder and black pepper over mixture in bowl, then spoon into ungreased air fryer basket. 3. Adjust the temperature to 160ºC and air fry for 12 minutes. Shake basket halfway through cooking. Radishes will be tender when done. Serve warm.

Courgette Balls

Prep time: 5 minutes | Cook time: 10 minutes |
Serves 4

4 courgettes
1 egg
45 g grated Parmesan cheese

1 tablespoon Italian herbs
75 g grated coconut

1. Thinly grate the courgettes and dry with a cheesecloth, ensuring to remove all the moisture. 2. In a bowl, combine the courgettes with the egg, Parmesan, Italian herbs, and grated coconut, mixing well to incorporate everything. Using the hands, mold the mixture into balls. 3. Preheat the air fryer to 200ºC. 4. Lay the courgette balls in one of the air fryer baskets and air fry for 10 minutes. 5. Serve hot.

Indian Aubergine Bharta

Prep time: 15 minutes | Cook time: 20 minutes | Serves 4

1 medium aubergine
2 tablespoons vegetable oil
25 g finely minced onion
100 g finely chopped fresh tomato

2 tablespoons fresh lemon juice
2 tablespoons chopped fresh coriander
½ teaspoon coarse sea salt
⅛ teaspoon cayenne pepper

1. Rub the aubergine all over with the vegetable oil. Place the aubergine in one of the air fryer baskets. Set the air fryer to 200°C for 20 minutes, or until the aubergine skin is blistered and charred. 2. Transfer the aubergine to a re-sealable plastic bag, seal, and set aside for 15 to 20 minutes (the aubergine will finish cooking in the residual heat trapped in the bag). 3. Transfer the aubergine to a large bowl. Peel off and discard the charred skin. Roughly mash the aubergine flesh. Add the onion, tomato, lemon juice, coriander, salt, and cayenne. Stir to combine.

Caramelized Aubergine with Harissa Yogurt

Prep time: 10 minutes | Cook time: 15 minutes | Serves 2

1 medium aubergine (about 340 g), cut crosswise into ½-inch-thick slices and quartered
2 tablespoons vegetable oil
coarse sea salt and freshly ground black pepper, to taste

120 g plain yogurt (not Greek)
2 tablespoons harissa paste
1 garlic clove, grated
2 teaspoons honey

1. In a bowl, toss together the aubergine and oil, season with salt and pepper, and toss to coat evenly. Transfer to the air fryer and air fry at 200°C, shaking the basket every 5 minutes, until the aubergine is caramelized and tender, about 15 minutes. 2. Meanwhile, in a small bowl, whisk together the yogurt, harissa, and garlic, then spread onto a serving plate. 3. Pile the warm aubergine over the yogurt and drizzle with the honey just before serving.

Chapter 8 Vegetarian Mains

Chapter 8 Vegetarian Mains

Cauliflower Steak with Gremolata

Prep time: 15 minutes | Cook time: 25 minutes |

Serves 4

2 tablespoons olive oil	60 g Parmesan cheese
1 tablespoon Italian seasoning	Gremolata:
1 large head cauliflower, outer	1 bunch Italian parsley
leaves removed and sliced	2 cloves garlic
lengthwise through the core	Zest of 1 small lemon, plus 1 to
into thick "steaks"	2 teaspoons lemon juice
Salt and freshly ground black	120 ml olive oil
pepper, to taste	Salt and pepper, to taste

1. Preheat the air fryer to 200ºC. 2.In a small bowl, combine the olive oil and Italian seasoning. 3.Brush both sides of each cauliflower "steak" generously with the oil. 4.Season to taste with salt and black pepper. 5.Working in batches if necessary, arrange the cauliflower in a single layer in one of the air fryer baskets. 6.Pausing halfway through the cooking time to turn the "steaks," air fry for 15 to 20 minutes until the cauliflower is tender and the edges begin to brown. 7.Sprinkle with the Parmesan and air fry for 5 minutes longer. 8.To make the gremolata: In a food processor fitted with a metal blade, combine the parsley, garlic, and lemon zest and juice. 9.With the motor running, add the olive oil in a steady stream until the mixture forms a bright green sauce. 10.Season to taste with salt and black pepper. 11.Serve the cauliflower steaks with the gremolata spooned over the top.

Super Vegetable Burger

Prep time: 15 minutes | Cook time: 12 minutes |

Serves 8

230 g cauliflower, steamed and	tablespoons water, divided
diced, rinsed and drained	1 teaspoon mustard powder
2 teaspoons coconut oil, melted	2 teaspoons thyme
2 teaspoons minced garlic	2 teaspoons parsley
60 g desiccated coconut	2 teaspoons chives
120 g oats	Salt and ground black pepper,
3 tablespoons flour	to taste
1 tablespoon flaxseeds plus 3	235 g breadcrumbs

1. Preheat the air fryer to 200ºC. 2.Combine the cauliflower with all the ingredients, except for the breadcrumbs, incorporating everything well. 3.Using the hands, shape 8 equal-sized amounts of the mixture into burger patties. 4.Coat the patties in breadcrumbs before putting them half in zone 1, the remaining in zone 2 in a single layer. 5.Air fry for 12 minutes or until crispy. 6.Serve hot.

Teriyaki Cauliflower

Prep time: 5 minutes | Cook time: 14 minutes |

Serves 4

120 ml soy sauce	2 cloves garlic, chopped
80 ml water	½ teaspoon chilli powder
1 tablespoon brown sugar	1 big cauliflower head, cut into
1 teaspoon sesame oil	florets
1 teaspoon cornflour	

1. Preheat the air fryer to 170ºC. 2.Make the teriyaki sauce: In a small bowl, whisk together the soy sauce, water, brown sugar, sesame oil, cornflour, garlic, and chilli powder until well combined. 3.Place the cauliflower florets in a large bowl and drizzle the top with the prepared teriyaki sauce and toss to coat well. 4.Put the cauliflower florets in one of the air fryer baskets and air fry for 14 minutes, shaking the basket halfway through, or until the cauliflower is crisp-tender. 5.Let the cauliflower cool for 5 minutes before serving.

Cheese Stuffed Peppers

Prep time: 20 minutes | Cook time: 15 minutes |

Serves 2

1 red pepper, top and seeds	Salt and pepper, to taste
removed	235 g Cottage cheese
1 yellow pepper, top and seeds	4 tablespoons mayonnaise
removed	2 pickles, chopped

1. Arrange the peppers in the lightly greased air fryer basket. 2.Cook in the preheated air fryer at 200ºC for 15 minutes, turning them over halfway through the cooking time. 3.Season with salt and pepper. 4.Then, in a mixing bowl, combine the soft white cheese with the mayonnaise and chopped pickles. 5.Stuff the pepper with the soft white cheese mixture and serve. 6.Enjoy!

Super Veg Rolls

Prep time: 20 minutes | Cook time: 10 minutes |

Serves 6

2 potatoes, mashed

60 g peas

60 g mashed carrots

1 small cabbage, sliced

60 g beans

2 tablespoons sweetcorn

1 small onion, chopped

120 g breadcrumbs

1 packet spring roll sheets

120 g cornflour slurry (mix 40 g cornflour with 80 ml water)

1. Preheat the air fryer to 200ºC. 2.Boil all the vegetables in water over a low heat. 3.Rinse and allow to dry. 4.Unroll the spring roll sheets and spoon equal amounts of vegetable onto the centre of each one. 5.Fold into spring rolls and coat each one with the slurry and breadcrumbs. 6.Air fry the rolls half in zone 1, the remaining in zone 2, for 10 minutes. 7.Serve warm.

Italian Baked Egg and Veggies & Roasted Vegetable Mélange with Herbs

Prep time: 20 minutes | Cook time: 18 minutes

Italian Baked Egg and Veggies | Serves 2:

2 tablespoons salted butter

1 small courgette, sliced lengthwise and quartered

½ medium green pepper, seeded and diced

235 g fresh spinach, chopped

1 medium plum tomato, diced

2 large eggs

¼ teaspoon onion powder

¼ teaspoon garlic powder

½ teaspoon dried basil

¼ teaspoon dried oregano

Roasted Vegetable Mélange with Herbs | Serves 4:

1 (230 g) package sliced mushrooms

1 yellow butternut squash, sliced

1 red pepper, sliced

3 cloves garlic, sliced

1 tablespoon olive oil

½ teaspoon dried basil

½ teaspoon dried thyme

½ teaspoon dried tarragon

Prepare for Italian Baked Egg and Veggies:

1. Grease two ramekins with 1 tablespoon butter each.

2.In a large bowl, toss courgette, pepper, spinach, and tomato.

3.Divide the mixture in two and place half in each ramekin.

4.Crack an egg on top of each ramekin and sprinkle with onion powder, garlic powder, basil, and oregano.

5.Place into zone 1.

Prepare for Roasted Vegetable Mélange with Herbs:

1. Preheat the air fryer to 180ºC.

2.Toss the mushrooms, squash, and pepper with the garlic and olive oil in a large bowl until well coated.

3.Mix in the basil, thyme, and tarragon and toss again.

4.Spread the vegetables evenly in zone 2.

Cook:

1. In zone 1, adjust the air fryer temperature to 170ºC and air fry for 10 minutes, or until the vegetables are fork-tender.

2. In zone 2, adjust the air fryer temperature to 170ºC and air fry for 14 to 18 minutes.

3. Press SYNC, then press Start.

4. For zone 2, cool for 5 minutes before serving.

Pesto Spinach Flatbread

Prep time: 10 minutes | Cook time: 8 minutes |

Serves 4

235 g blanched finely ground almond flour

60 g soft white cheese

475 g shredded Mozzarella

cheese

235 g chopped fresh spinach leaves

2 tablespoons basil pesto

1. Place flour, soft white cheese, and Mozzarella in a large microwave-safe bowl and microwave on high 45 seconds, then stir. 2.Fold in spinach and microwave an additional 15 seconds. 3.Stir until a soft dough ball forms. 4.Cut two pieces of parchment paper to fit air fryer basket. 5.Separate dough into two sections and press each out on ungreased parchment to create 6-inch rounds. 6.Spread 1 tablespoon pesto over each flatbread and place rounds on parchment into ungreased air fryer basket. 7.Adjust the temperature to 180ºC and air fry for 8 minutes, turning crusts halfway through cooking. 8.Flatbread will be golden when done. 9.Let cool 5 minutes before slicing and serving.

Whole Roasted Lemon Cauliflower

Prep time: 5 minutes | Cook time: 15 minutes |

Serves 4

1 medium head cauliflower

2 tablespoons salted butter, melted

1 medium lemon

½ teaspoon garlic powder

1 teaspoon dried parsley

1. Remove the leaves from the head of cauliflower and brush it with melted butter. 2.Cut the lemon in half and zest one half onto the cauliflower. 3.Squeeze the juice of the zested lemon half and pour it over the cauliflower. 4.Sprinkle with garlic powder and parsley. 5.Place cauliflower head into one of the air fryer baskets. 6.Adjust the temperature to 180ºC and air fry for 15 minutes. 7.Check cauliflower every 5 minutes to avoid overcooking. 8.It should be fork tender. To serve, squeeze juice from other lemon half over cauliflower. 9.Serve immediately.

Garlicky Sesame Carrots

Prep time: 5 minutes | Cook time: 16 minutes | Serves 4 to 6

450 g baby carrots
1 tablespoon sesame oil
½ teaspoon dried dill
Pinch salt

Freshly ground black pepper, to taste
6 cloves garlic, peeled
3 tablespoons sesame seeds

1. Preheat the air fryer to 190°C. 2.In a medium bowl, drizzle the baby carrots with the sesame oil. 3.Sprinkle with the dill, salt, and pepper and toss to coat well. 4.Place the baby carrots in the air fryer basket and roast for 8 minutes. 5.Remove the basket and stir in the garlic. 6.Return the basket to the air fryer and roast for another 8 minutes, or until the carrots are lightly browned. 7.Serve sprinkled with the sesame seeds.

Chapter 9 Family Favorites

Chapter 9 Family Favorites

Chinese-Inspired Spareribs

Prep time: 30 minutes | Cook time: 8 minutes | Serves 4

Oil, for spraying	120 g beef broth
340 g pork ribs, cut into 3-inch-long pieces	60 ml honey
	2 tablespoons minced garlic
235 ml soy sauce	1 teaspoon ground ginger
140 g sugar	2 drops red food dye (optional)

1. Line one of the air fryer baskets with parchment and spray lightly with oil. 2.Combine the ribs, soy sauce, sugar, beef broth, honey, garlic, ginger, and food colouring (if using) in a large zip-top plastic bag, seal, and shake well until completely coated. 3.Refrigerate for at least 30 minutes. 4.Place the ribs in the prepared basket. 5.Air fry at 190°C for 8 minutes, or until the internal temperature reaches 74°C.

Scallops with Green Vegetables

Prep time: 15 minutes | Cook time: 8 to 11 minutes | Serves 4

235 g green beans	½ teaspoon dried basil
235 g garden peas	½ teaspoon dried oregano
235 g frozen chopped broccoli	340 g sea scallops
2 teaspoons olive oil	

1. In a large bowl, toss the green beans, peas, and broccoli with the olive oil. 2.Place in one of the air fryer baskets. 3.Air fry at 200°C for 4 to 6 minutes, or until the vegetables are crisp-tender. 4.Remove the vegetables from one of the air fryer baskets and sprinkle with the herbs. Set aside. 5.In the air fryer basket, put the scallops and air fry for 4 to 5 minutes, or until the scallops are firm and reach an internal temperature of just 64°C on a meat thermometer. 6.Toss scallops with the vegetables and serve immediately.

Veggie Tuna Melts

Prep time: 15 minutes | Cook time: 7 to 11 minutes | Serves 4

2 low-salt wholemeal English muffins, split	green parts, sliced
	80 ml fat-free Greek yoghurt
1 (170 g) can chunk light low-salt tuna, drained	2 tablespoons low-salt wholegrain mustard
235 g shredded carrot	2 slices low-salt low-fat Swiss cheese, halved
80 g chopped mushrooms	
2 spring onions, white and	

1. Place the English muffin halves in one of the air fryer baskets. 2.Air fry at 170°C for 3 to 4 minutes, or until crisp. Remove from the basket and set aside. 3.In a medium bowl, thoroughly mix the tuna, carrot, mushrooms, spring onions, yoghurt, and mustard. 4.Top each half of the muffins with one-fourth of the tuna mixture and a half slice of Swiss cheese. 5.Air fry for 4 to 7 minutes, or until the tuna mixture is hot and the cheese melts and starts to brown. 6.Serve immediately.

Old Bay Tilapia

Prep time: 15 minutes | Cook time: 6 minutes | Serves 4

Oil, for spraying	½ teaspoon salt
235 ml panko breadcrumbs	¼ teaspoon freshly ground black pepper
2 tablespoons Old Bay or all-purpose seasoning	
2 teaspoons granulated garlic	1 large egg
1 teaspoon onion powder	4 tilapia fillets

1. Preheat the air fryer to 204°C. 2. Line one of the air fryer baskets with parchment and spray lightly with oil. 3. In a shallow bowl, mix together the breadcrumbs, seasoning, garlic, onion powder, salt, and black pepper. 4. In a small bowl, whisk the egg. 5. Coat the tilapia in the egg, then dredge in the bread crumb mixture until completely coated. 6. Place the tilapia in the prepared basket. You may need to work in batches, depending on the size of your air fryer. Spray lightly with oil. 7. Cook for 4 to 6 minutes, depending on the thickness of the fillets, until the internal temperature reaches 64°C. 8. Serve immediately.

Meringue Cookies

Prep time: 15 minutes | Cook time: 1 hour 30 minutes | Makes 20 cookies

Oil, for spraying
4 large egg whites

185 g sugar
Pinch cream of tartar

1. Preheat the air fryer to 60ºC. 2.Line the air fryer basket with parchment and spray lightly with oil. 3.In a small heatproof bowl, whisk together the egg whites and sugar. 4.Fill a small saucepan halfway with water, place it over medium heat, and bring to a light simmer. 5.Place the bowl with the egg whites on the saucepan, making sure the bottom of the bowl does not touch the water. 6.Whisk the mixture until the sugar is dissolved. Transfer the mixture to a large bowl and add the cream of tartar. 7.Using an electric mixer, beat the mixture on high until it is glossy and stiff peaks form. 8.Transfer the mixture to a piping bag or a zip-top plastic bag with a corner cut off. Pipe rounds into the prepared basket. 9.You may need to work in batches, depending on the size of your air fryer. Cook for 1 hour 30 minutes. 10.Turn off the air fryer and let the meringues cool completely inside. 11.The residual heat will continue to dry them out.

Filo Vegetable Triangles

Prep time: 15 minutes | Cook time: 6 to 11 minutes | Serves 6

3 tablespoons finely chopped onion
2 garlic cloves, minced
2 tablespoons grated carrot
1 teaspoon olive oil
3 tablespoons frozen baby peas, thawed

2 tablespoons fat-free soft white cheese, at room temperature
6 sheets frozen filo pastry, thawed
Olive oil spray, for coating the dough

1. In a baking pan, combine the onion, garlic, carrot, and olive oil. 2.Air fry at 200ºC for 2 to 4 minutes, or until the vegetables are crisp-tender. 3.Transfer to a bowl. 4.Stir in the peas and soft white cheese to the vegetable mixture. Let cool while you prepare the dough. 5.Lay one sheet of filo on a work surface and lightly spray with olive oil spray. 6.Top with another sheet of filo. Repeat with the remaining 4 filo sheets; you'll have 3 stacks with 2 layers each. 7.Cut each stack lengthwise into 4 strips (12 strips total). Place a scant 2 teaspoons of the filling near the bottom of each strip. 8.Bring one corner up over the filling to make a triangle; continue folding the triangles over, as you would fold a flag. 9.Seal the edge with a bit of water. Repeat with the remaining strips and filling. 10.Air fry the triangles, in 2 batches, for 4 to 7 minutes, or until golden brown. Serve.

Mixed Berry Crumble

Prep time: 10 minutes | Cook time: 11 to 16 minutes | Serves 4

120 g chopped fresh strawberries
120 g fresh blueberries
80 g frozen raspberries
1 tablespoon freshly squeezed lemon juice

1 tablespoon honey
80 g wholemeal plain flour
3 tablespoons light muscovado sugar
2 tablespoons unsalted butter, melted

1. In a baking pan, combine the strawberries, blueberries, and raspberries. 2.Drizzle with the lemon juice and honey. 3.In a small bowl, mix the pastry flour and brown sugar. 4.Stir in the butter and mix until crumbly. 5.Sprinkle this mixture over the fruit. 6.Bake at 190ºC for 11 to 16 minutes, or until the fruit is tender and bubbly and the topping is golden brown. 7.Serve warm.

Meatball Subs

Prep time: 15 minutes | Cook time: 19 minutes | Serves 6

Oil, for spraying
450 g 15% fat minced beef
120 ml Italian breadcrumbs (mixed breadcrumbs, Italian seasoning and salt)
1 tablespoon dried minced onion
1 tablespoon minced garlic

1 large egg
1 teaspoon salt
1 teaspoon freshly ground black pepper
6 sub rolls
1 (510 g) jar marinara sauce
350 ml shredded Mozzarella cheese

1. Preheat the air fryer to 200ºC. Lightly spray zone 1 with oil. 2. In a large bowl, combine the minced beef, Italian breadcrumbs, dried minced onion, minced garlic, egg, salt, and black pepper. Mix until well combined. 3. Shape the mixture into meatballs of your desired size. 4. Place the meatballs in zone 1 of the air fryer basket, ensuring they are evenly spaced. 5. In zone 2, place the sub rolls and lightly toast them. 6. Air fry for 15 minutes, flipping the meatballs halfway through the cooking time. 7. While the meatballs are cooking, warm the marinara sauce in a saucepan or microwave. 8. Once the meatballs are cooked, remove them from zone 1 and place them in the marinara sauce. Stir to coat the meatballs evenly. 9. Place a few meatballs with sauce onto each toasted sub roll. 10. Top the meatballs with shredded Mozzarella cheese. 11. Return the sub rolls to zone 2 of the air fryer and air fry for 4 minutes, or until the cheese is melted and bubbly. 12. Remove from the air fryer and serve the meatball subs hot.

Steak and Vegetable Kebabs

Prep time: 15 minutes | Cook time: 5 to 7 minutes | Serves 4

2 tablespoons balsamic vinegar

2 teaspoons olive oil

½ teaspoon dried marjoram

⅛ teaspoon ground black pepper

340 g silverside, cut into 1-inch pieces

1 red pepper, sliced

16 button mushrooms

235 g cherry tomatoes

1. In a medium bowl, stir together the balsamic vinegar, olive oil, marjoram, and black pepper. 2.Add the steak and stir to coat. Let stand for 10 minutes at room temperature. 3.Alternating items, thread the beef, red pepper, mushrooms, and tomatoes onto 8 bamboo or metal skewers that fit in the air fryer. 4.Air fry at 200ºC for 5 to 7 minutes, or until the beef is browned and reaches at least 64ºC on a meat thermometer. 5.Serve immediately.

Pecan Rolls

Prep time: 20 minutes | Cook time: 20 to 24 minutes | Makes 12 rolls

220 g plain flour, plus more for dusting

2 tablespoons caster sugar, plus 60 ml, divided

1 teaspoon salt

3 tablespoons butter, at room temperature

180 ml milk, whole or semi-skimmed

40 g packed light muscovado sugar

120g chopped pecans, toasted

1 to 2 tablespoons oil

35g icing sugar (optional)

1. In a large bowl, whisk the flour, 2 tablespoons caster sugar, and salt until blended. 2.Stir in the butter and milk briefly until a sticky dough form. In a small bowl, stir together the brown sugar and remaining 60 g caster sugar. 3.Place a piece of parchment paper on a work surface and dust it with flour. Roll the dough on the prepared surface to ¼ inch thickness. 4.Spread the sugar mixture over the dough. Sprinkle the pecans on top. Roll up the dough jelly roll-style, pinching the ends to seal. 5.Cut the dough into 12 rolls. Preheat the air fryer to 160ºC. 6.Line the air fryer basket with parchment paper and spritz the parchment with oil. Place 6 rolls on the prepared parchment. Bake for 5 minutes. 7.Flip the rolls and bake for 5 to 7 minutes more until lightly browned. Repeat with the remaining rolls. 8.Sprinkle with icing sugar (if using).

Chapter 10 Fast and Easy Everyday Favourites

Chapter 10 Fast and Easy Everyday Favourites

Beery and Crunchy Onion Rings

Prep time: 10 minutes | Cook time: 16 minutes |
Serves 2 to 4

80 g plain flour	180 ml beer
1 teaspoon paprika	175 g breadcrumbs
½ teaspoon bicarbonate of soda	1 tablespoons olive oil
1 teaspoon salt	1 large Vidalia or sweet onion,
½ teaspoon freshly ground	peeled and sliced into ½-inch
black pepper	rings
1 egg, beaten	Cooking spray

1. Preheat the air fryer to 180°C. 2. Spritz one of the air fryer baskets with cooking spray. 3. Combine the flour, paprika, bicarbonate of soda, salt, and ground black pepper in a bowl. Stir to mix well. 4. Combine the egg and beer in a separate bowl. Stir to mix well. 5. Make a well in the centre of the flour mixture, then pour the egg mixture in the well. Stir to mix everything well. 6. Pour the breadcrumbs and olive oil in a shallow plate. Stir to mix well. 7. Dredge the onion rings gently into the flour and egg mixture, then shake the excess off and put into the plate of breadcrumbs. 8. Flip to coat both sides well. Arrange the onion rings in the preheated air fryer. 9. Air fry in batches for 16 minutes or until golden brown and crunchy. 10. Flip the rings and put the bottom rings to the top halfway through. 11. Serve immediately.

Buttery Sweet Potatoes

Prep time: 5 minutes | Cook time: 10 minutes |
Serves 4

2 tablespoons melted butter	into ½-inch cubes
1 tablespoon light brown sugar	Cooking spray
2 sweet potatoes, peeled and cut	

1. Preheat the air fryer to 200°C. 2. Line one of the air fryer baskets with parchment paper. In a medium bowl, stir together the melted butter and brown sugar until blended. 3. Toss the sweet potatoes in the butter mixture until coated. Place the sweet potatoes on the parchment and spritz with oil. 4. Air fry for 5 minutes. Shake the basket, spritz the sweet potatoes with oil, and air fry for 5 minutes more until they're soft enough to cut with a fork. 5. Serve immediately.

Easy Devils on Horseback

Prep time: 5 minutes | Cook time: 7 minutes | Serves
12

24 small pitted prunes (128 g)	8 slices centre-cut bacon, cut
60 g crumbled blue cheese,	crosswise into thirds
divided	

1. Preheat the air fryer to 200°C. 2. Halve the prunes lengthwise, but don't cut them all the way through. 3. Place ½ teaspoon of cheese in the centre of each prune. 4. Wrap a piece of bacon around each prune and secure the bacon with a toothpick. 5. Working in batches, arrange a single layer of the prunes in the air fryer basket. 6. Air fry for about 7 minutes, flipping halfway, until the bacon is cooked through and crisp. 7. Let cool slightly and serve warm.

Indian-Style Sweet Potato Fries

Prep time: 5 minutes | Cook time: 8 minutes | Makes
20 fries

Seasoning Mixture:	¼ teaspoon ground cayenne
¾ teaspoon ground coriander	pepper
½ teaspoon garam masala	Fries:
½ teaspoon garlic powder	2 large sweet potatoes, peeled
½ teaspoon ground cumin	2 teaspoons olive oil

1. Preheat the air fryer to 200°C. 2. In a small bowl, combine the coriander, garam masala, garlic powder, cumin, and cayenne pepper. 3. Slice the sweet potatoes into ¼-inch-thick fries. In a large bowl, toss the sliced sweet potatoes with the olive oil and the seasoning mixture. 4. Transfer the seasoned sweet potatoes to one of the air fryer baskets and fry for 8 minutes, until crispy. 5. Serve warm.

Spinach and Carrot Balls

Prep time: 10 minutes | Cook time: 10 minutes | Serves 4

2 slices toasted bread	1 teaspoon minced garlic
1 carrot, peeled and grated	1 teaspoon salt
1 package fresh spinach, blanched and chopped	½ teaspoon black pepper
½ onion, chopped	1 tablespoon Engevita yeast flakes
1 egg, beaten	1 tablespoon flour
½ teaspoon garlic powder	

1. Preheat the air fryer to 200ºC. 2. In a food processor, pulse the toasted bread to form breadcrumbs. 3. Transfer into a shallow dish or bowl. In a bowl, mix together all the other ingredients. 4. Use your hands to shape the mixture into small-sized balls. 5. Roll the balls in the breadcrumbs, ensuring to cover them well. 6. Put in one of the air fryer baskets and air fry for 10 minutes. 7. Serve immediately.

Air Fried Shishito Peppers

Prep time: 5 minutes | Cook time: 5 minutes | Serves 4

230 g shishito or Padron peppers (about 24)	Coarse sea salt, to taste
1 tablespoon olive oil	Lemon wedges, for serving
	Cooking spray

1. Preheat the air fryer to 200ºC. 2. Spritz one of the air fryer baskets with cooking spray. 3. Toss the peppers with olive oil in a large bowl to coat well. Arrange the peppers in the preheated air fryer. 4. Air fryer for 5 minutes or until blistered and lightly charred. Shake the basket and sprinkle the peppers with salt halfway through the cooking time. 5. Transfer the peppers onto a plate and squeeze the lemon wedges on top before serving.

Corn Fritters

Prep time: 15 minutes | Cook time: 8 minutes | Serves 6

120 g self-raising flour	60 g buttermilk
1 tablespoon sugar	180 g corn kernels
1 teaspoon salt	60 g minced onion
1 large egg, lightly beaten	Cooking spray

1. Preheat the air fryer to 180ºC. 2. Line the air fryer basket with parchment paper. In a medium bowl, whisk the flour, sugar, and salt until blended. Stir in the egg and buttermilk. 3. Add the corn and minced onion. 4. Mix well. Shape the corn fritter batter into 12 balls. 5. Place the fritters on the parchment and spritz with oil. Bake for 4 minutes. 6. Flip the fritters, spritz them with oil, and bake for 4 minutes more until firm and lightly browned. 7. Serve immediately.

Bacon Pinwheels

Prep time: 10 minutes | Cook time: 10 minutes | Makes 8 pinwheels

1 sheet puff pastry	8 slices bacon
2 tablespoons maple syrup	Ground black pepper, to taste
48 g brown sugar	Cooking spray

1. Preheat the air fryer to 180ºC. 2. Spritz one of the air fryer baskets with cooking spray. 3. Roll the puff pastry into a 10-inch square with a rolling pin on a clean work surface, then cut the pastry into 8 strips. 4. Brush the strips with maple syrup and sprinkle with sugar, leaving a 1-inch far end uncovered. 5. Arrange each slice of bacon on each strip, leaving a ⅛-inch length of bacon hang over the end close to you. 6. Sprinkle with black pepper. 7. From the end close to you, roll the strips into pinwheels, then dab the uncovered end with water and seal the rolls. 8. Arrange the pinwheels in the preheated air fryer and spritz with cooking spray. 9. Air fry for 10 minutes or until golden brown. 10. Flip the pinwheels halfway through. 11. Serve immediately.

Peppery Brown Rice Fritters

Prep time: 10 minutes | Cook time: 8 to 10 minutes | Serves 4

1 (284 g) bag frozen cooked brown rice, thawed	2 tablespoons minced fresh basil
1 egg	3 tablespoons grated Parmesan cheese
3 tablespoons brown rice flour	2 teaspoons olive oil
80 g finely grated carrots	
80 g minced red pepper	

1. Preheat the air fryer to 190ºC. 2. In a small bowl, combine the thawed rice, egg, and flour and mix to blend. 3. Stir in the carrots, pepper, basil, and Parmesan cheese. 4. Form the mixture into 8 fritters and drizzle with the olive oil. 5. Put the fritters carefully into one of the air fryer baskets. 6. Air fry for 8 to 10 minutes, or until the fritters are golden brown and cooked through. 7. Serve immediately.

Cheesy Chilli Toast

Prep time: 5 minutes | Cook time: 5 minutes | Serves 1

2 tablespoons grated Parmesan cheese
2 tablespoons grated Mozzarella cheese
2 teaspoons salted butter, at room temperature
10 to 15 thin slices serrano chilli or jalapeño
2 slices sourdough bread
½ teaspoon black pepper

1. Preheat the air fryer to 160ºC. 2. In a small bowl, stir together the Parmesan, Mozzarella, butter, and chillies. 3. Spread half the mixture onto one side of each slice of bread. 4. Sprinkle with the pepper. 5. Place the slices, cheese-side up, in one of the air fryer baskets. 6. Bake for 5 minutes, or until the cheese has melted and started to brown slightly. 7. Serve immediately.

Cheesy Jalapeño Cornbread

Prep time: 10 minutes | Cook time: 20 minutes | Serves 8

160 ml cornmeal
80 ml plain flour
¾ teaspoon baking powder
2 tablespoons margarine, melted
½ teaspoon rock salt
1 tablespoon granulated sugar
180 ml whole milk
1 large egg, beaten
1 jalapeño pepper, thinly sliced
80 ml shredded extra mature Cheddar cheese
Cooking spray

1. Preheat the air fryer to 152ºC. Spritz the air fryer basket with cooking spray. 2. Combine all the ingredients in a large bowl. Stir to mix well. Pour the mixture in a baking pan. 3. Arrange the pan in the preheated air fryer. Bake for 20 minutes or until a toothpick inserted in the centre of the bread comes out clean. 4. When the cooking is complete, remove the baking pan from the air fryer and allow the bread to cool for a few minutes before slicing to serve.

Herb-Roasted Veggies

Prep time: 10 minutes | Cook time: 14 to 18 minutes | Serves 4

1 red pepper, sliced
1 (230 g) package sliced mushrooms
235 g green beans, cut into 2-inch pieces
80 g diced red onion
3 garlic cloves, sliced
1 teaspoon olive oil
½ teaspoon dried basil
½ teaspoon dried tarragon

1. Preheat the air fryer to 180ºC. 2. In a medium bowl, mix the red pepper, mushrooms, green beans, red onion, and garlic. 3. Drizzle with the olive oil. Toss to coat. 4. Add the herbs and toss again. Place the vegetables in one of the air fryer baskets. 5. Roast for 14 to 18 minutes, or until tender. 6. Serve immediately.

Cheesy Potato Patties

Prep time: 5 minutes | Cook time: 10 minutes | Serves 8

900 g white potatoes
120 g finely chopped spring onions
½ teaspoon freshly ground black pepper, or more to taste
1 tablespoon fine sea salt
½ teaspoon hot paprika
475 g shredded Colby or Monterey Jack cheese
60 ml rapeseed oil
235 g crushed crackers

1. Preheat the air fryer to 180ºC. Boil the potatoes until soft. 2. Dry them off and peel them before mashing thoroughly, leaving no lumps. 3. Combine the mashed potatoes with spring onions, pepper, salt, paprika, and cheese. 4. Mould the mixture into balls with your hands and press with your palm to flatten them into patties. 5. In a shallow dish, combine the rapeseed oil and crushed crackers. 6. Coat the patties in the crumb mixture. 7. Bake the patties for about 10 minutes, in multiple batches if necessary. 8. Serve hot.

Purple Potato Chips with Rosemary

Prep time: 10 minutes | Cook time: 9 to 14 minutes | Serves 6

235 ml Greek yoghurt
2 chipotle chillies, minced
2 tablespoons adobo or chipotle sauce
1 teaspoon paprika
1 tablespoon lemon juice
10 purple fingerling or miniature potatoes
1 teaspoon olive oil
2 teaspoons minced fresh rosemary leaves
⅛ teaspoon cayenne pepper
¼ teaspoon coarse sea salt

1. Preheat the air fryer to 200ºC. 2. In a medium bowl, combine the yoghurt, minced chillies, adobo sauce, paprika, and lemon juice. Mix well and refrigerate. 3. Wash the potatoes and dry them with paper towels. 4. Slice the potatoes lengthwise, as thinly as possible. You can use a mandoline, a vegetable peeler, or a very sharp knife. 5. Combine the potato slices in a medium bowl and drizzle with the olive oil; toss to coat. 6. Air fry the chips, in batches, half in zone 1, the remaining in zone 2, for 9 to 14 minutes. 7. Use tongs to gently rearrange the chips halfway during cooking time. 8. Sprinkle the chips with the rosemary, cayenne pepper, and sea salt. 9. Serve with the chipotle sauce for dipping.

Sweet Corn and Carrot Fritters

Prep time: 10 minutes | Cook time: 8 to 11 minutes | Serves 4

1 medium-sized carrot, grated

1 yellow onion, finely chopped

4 ounces (113 g) canned sweet corn kernels, drained

1 teaspoon sea salt flakes

1 tablespoon chopped fresh cilantro

1 medium-sized egg, whisked

2 tablespoons plain milk

1 cup grated Parmesan cheese

¼ cup flour

⅓ teaspoon baking powder

⅓ teaspoon sugar

Cooking spray

1. Preheat the air fryer to 350ºF (177ºC). 2. Place the grated carrot in a colander and press down to squeeze out any excess moisture. Dry it with a paper towel. 3. Combine the carrots with the remaining ingredients. 4. Mold 1 tablespoon of the mixture into a ball and press it down with your hand or a spoon to flatten it. Repeat until the rest of the mixture is used up. 5. Spritz the balls with cooking spray. 6. Arrange in one of the air fryer baskets, taking care not to overlap any balls. Bake for 8 to 11 minutes, or until they're firm. 7. Serve warm.

Printed in Great Britain
by Amazon

34175301R00042